ANNIE HALL

Annie Hall

Screenplay by Woody Allen
and Marshall Brickman

ff

faber and faber

First published in the USA in 1982
as Four Films of Woody Allen
by Random House, Inc., New York
First published in Great Britain in 1983
by Faber and Faber Limited
3 Queen Square London WC1N 3AU
Reprinted 1988 and 1991
This edition published in 2000
Printed in Great Britain by
Mackays of Chatham plc, Chatham, Kent

Photos: Brian Hamil/Photoreporters

A CIP record for this book
is available from the British Library

ISBN 0-571-20214-4

2 4 6 8 10 9 7 5 3 1

THE ITALICIZED PASSAGES THAT DESCRIBE THE ACTION
HAVE BEEN PROVIDED BY THE PUBLISHER.

Annie Hall

United Artists

United Artists Company
A Transamerica Company

ANNIE HALL

A JACK ROLLINS–CHARLES H. JOFFE PRODUCTION

EDITED BY
RALPH ROSENBLUM, A.C.E.

ART DIRECTOR
MEL BOURNE

COSTUME DESIGNER
RUTH MORLEY

DIRECTOR OF PHOTOGRAPHY
GORDON WILLIS, A.S.C.

WRITTEN BY
WOODY ALLEN AND MARSHALL BRICKMAN

PRODUCED BY
CHARLES H. JOFFE

DIRECTED BY
WOODY ALLEN

(Sound and Woody Allen monologue begin)

FADE IN:

White credits dissolve in and out on black screen. No sound.

FADE OUT credits

FADE IN:

Abrupt medium close-up of Alvy Singer doing a comedy monologue. He's wearing a crumbled sports jacket and tieless shirt; the background is stark.

ALVY There's an old joke. Uh, two elderly women are at a Catskills mountain resort, and one of 'em says: "Boy, the food at this place is really terrible." The other one says, "Yeah, I know, and such ... small portions." Well, that's essentially how I feel about life. Full of loneliness and misery and suffering and unhappiness, and it's all over much too quickly. The—the other important joke for me is one that's, uh, usually attributed to Groucho Marx, but I think it appears originally in Freud's wit and its relation to the unconscious. And it goes like this—I'm paraphrasing: Uh . . . "I would never wanna belong to any club that would have someone like me for a member." That's the key joke of my adult life in terms of my relationships with women. Tsch, you know, lately the strangest things have been going through my mind, 'cause I turned forty, tsch, and I guess I'm going through a life crisis or something, I don't know. I, uh . . . and I'm not worried about aging. I'm not one o' those characters, you know. Although I'm balding slightly on top, that's about the worst you can say about me. I, uh, I think I'm gonna get better as I get older, you know? I think I'm gonna be the—the balding virile type, you know, as opposed to say the, uh, distinguished gray, for instance, you know? 'Less I'm neither o' those two. Unless I'm one o' those guys with saliva dribbling out of his mouth who wanders into a cafeteria with a shopping bag screaming about socialism. *(Sighing)* Annie and I broke up and I—I still can't get my mind around that. You know, I—I keep sifting the pieces o' the relationship through my mind and and —and examining my life and tryin' to figure out where did the screw-up come, you know, and a year ago we were . . . tsch, in love. You know, and-and-and . . . And it's funny, I'm not—I'm not a morose type. I'm not a depressive character. I-I-I, uh, *(Laughing)* you know, I was a reasonably happy kid, I guess. I was brought up in Brooklyn during World War II.

CUT TO:
INTERIOR. DOCTOR'S OFFICE—DAY.

Alvy as young boy sits on a sofa with his mother in an old-fashioned, cluttered doctor's office. The doctor stands near the sofa, holding a cigarette and listening.

MOTHER *(To the doctor)* He's been depressed. All off a sudden, he can't do anything.

DOCTOR *(Nodding)* Why are you depressed, Alvy?

MOTHER *(Nudging Alvy)* Tell Dr. Flicker. *(Young Alvy sits, his head down. His mother answers for him)* It's something he read.

DOCTOR *(Puffing on his cigarette and nodding)* Something he read, huh?

ALVY *(His head still down)* The universe is expanding.

DOCTOR The universe is expanding?

ALVY *(Looking up at the doctor)* Well, the universe is everything, and if it's expanding, someday it will break apart and that would be the end of everything!
Disgusted, his mother looks at him.

MOTHER *(Shouting)* What is that your business? *(She turns back to the doctor)* He stopped doing his homework.

ALVY What's the point?

MOTHER *(Excited, gesturing with her hands)* What has the universe got to do with it? You're here in Brooklyn! Brooklyn is not expanding!

DOCTOR *(Heartily, looking down at Alvy)* It won't be expanding for billions of years yet, Alvy. And we've gotta try to enjoy ourselves while we're here. Uh?
He laughs.

CUT TO:

Full shot of house with an amusement-park roller-coaster ride built over it. A line of cars move up and then slides with great speed while out the window of the house a hand shakes a dust mop.

ALVY'S VOICE   My analyst says I exaggerate my childhood memories, but I swear I was brought up underneath the roller—

CUT TO:
INTERIOR. HOUSE.

Alvy as a child sits at the table eating soup and reading a comic book while his father sits on the sofa reading the paper. The house shakes with every move of the roller coaster.

ALVY'S VOICE   —coaster in the Coney Island section of Brooklyn. Maybe that accounts for my personality, which is a little nervous, I think.

CUT TO:

Young Alvy at the food-stand concession watching three military men representing the Army, the Navy and the Marines arm in arm with a blond woman in a skirted bathing suit. They all turn and run toward the foreground. The girl stops before the camera to lean over and throw a kiss. The sign over the concession reads "Steve's Famous Clam Bar. Ice Cold Beer," and the roller coaster is moving in full gear in the background.

ALVY'S VOICE   You know, I have a hyperactive imagination. My mind tends to jump around a little, and I-I-I-I have some trouble between fantasy and reality.

CUT TO:

Full shot of people in bumper cars thoroughly enjoying bumping into each other as Alvy's father stands in the center of the track directing traffic.

ALVY'S VOICE   My father ran the bumper-car concession. *(Alvy as a child moves into the frame driving a bumper car. He stops as other cars bombard him. His father continues to direct the traffic)* There-there he is and there I am. But I-I-I-I used to get my aggression out through those cars all the time.
Alvy backs up his car offscreen.

INTERIOR. SCHOOLROOM—DAY.

The camera pans over three austere-looking teachers standing in front of the blackboard. The chalk writing on the board changes as each teacher lectures. While Alvy speaks, one of the male teachers puts an equation on the black-board: "2 × 10 = 20" and other arithmetic formulas.

ALVY'S VOICE   I remember the staff at our public school. You know, we had a saying, uh, that "Those who can't do, teach, and those who can't teach, teach gym." And . . . uh, h'h, of course, those who couldn't do anything, I think, were assigned to our school. I must say—

CUT TO:

A female teacher standing in front of an old-fashioned schoolroom. The blackboard behind her reads "Transportation Administration."
The camera pans her point of view: a group of young students sitting behind their desks. Alvy as a child sits in a center desk while all around him there is student activity; there is note-passing, ruler-tapping, nose-picking, gum-chewing.

ALVY'S VOICE   —I always felt my schoolmates were idiots. Melvyn Greenglass, you know, fat little face, and Henrietta Farrell, just Miss Perfect all the time. And-and Ivan Ackerman, always the wrong answer. Always.
Ivan stands up behind his desk.

IVAN   Seven and three is nine.
Alvy hits his forehead with his hand. Another student glances over at him, reacting.

ALVY'S VOICE   Even then I knew they were just jerks. *(The camera moves back to the teacher, who is glaring out at her students)* In nineteen forty-two I had already dis—
As Alvy talks, the camera shows him move from his seat and kiss a young girl. She jumps from her seat in disgust, rubbing her cheek, as Alvy moves back to his seat.

1ST GIRL *(Making noises)*   Ugh, he kissed me, he kissed me.

TEACHER *(Offscreen)*   That's the second time this month! Step up here!
As the teacher, really glaring now, speaks, Alvy rises from his seat and moves over to her. Angry, she points with her hand while the students turn their heads to watch what will happen next.

ALVY   What'd I do?

TEACHER   Step up here!

ALVY   What'd I do?

TEACHER   You should be ashamed of yourself!
The students, their heads still turned, look back at Alvy, now an adult, sitting in the last seat of the second row.

ALVY (AS ADULT) *(First offscreen, then onscreen as camera moves over to the back of the classroom)*   Why, I was just expressing a healthy sexual curiosity.

TEACHER *(The younger Alvy standing next to her)*   Six-year-old boys don't have girls on their minds.

ALVY (AS ADULT) *(Still sitting in the back of the classroom)*   I did.
The girl the young Alvy kissed turns to the older Alvy; she gestures and speaks.

1ST GIRL   For God's sakes, Alvy, even Freud speaks of a latency period.

ALVY (AS ADULT) *(Gesturing)*   Well, I never had a latency period. I can't help it.

TEACHER *(With young Alvy still at her side)*   Why couldn't you have been more like Donald? *(The camera pans over to Donald, sitting up tall in his seat, then back to the teacher)*   Now, there was a model boy!

ALVY (AS CHILD) *(Still standing next to the teacher)*   Tell the folks where you are today, Donald.

DONALD   I run a profitable dress company.

ALVY'S VOICE   Right. Sometimes I wonder where my classmates are today.
The camera shows the full classroom, the students sitting behind their desks, the teacher standing in the front of the room. One at a time, the young students rise up from their desks and speak.

1ST BOY   I'm president of the Pinkus Plumbing Company.

2ND BOY   I sell tallises.

3RD BOY   I used to be a heroin addict. Now I'm a methadone addict.

2ND GIRL   I'm into leather.

INTERIOR ROOM.

Close-up of a TV screen showing Alvy as an adult on a talk show. He sits next to the show's host, Dick Cavett, a Navy man sits on his right. Static is heard throughout the dialogue.

ALVY   I lost track of most of my old schoolmates, but I wound up a comedian. They did not take me in the Army. I was, uh . . . Interestingly enough, I was—I was four-P.
Sounds of TV audience laughter and applause are heard.

DICK CAVETT   Four-P?

ALVY   Yes. In-in-in-in the event of war, I'm a hostage.
More audience laughter joined by Dick Cavett and the naval officer.

INTERIOR. THE HOUSE WHERE ALVY GREW UP.

Alvy's mother sits at the old-fashioned dining-room table peeling carrots and talking as she looks offscreen.

MOTHER   You always only saw the worst in people. You never could get along with anyone at school. You were always outta step with the world. Even when you got famous, you still distrusted the world.

EXTERIOR. MANHATTAN. STREET—DAY.

A pretty Manhattan street with sidewalk trees, brownstones, a school; people mill about, some strolling and carrying bundles, others hurried. The screen shows the whole length of the sidewalk, a street, and part of the sidewalk beyond. As the following scene ensues, two pedestrians, indistinguishable in the distance, come closer and closer toward the camera, recognizable, finally, as Alvy and his best friend, Rob, deep in conversation. They eventually move past the camera and offscreen. Traffic noise is heard in the background.

ALVY   I distinctly heard it. He muttered under his breath, "Jew."

ROB   You're crazy!

ALVY   No, I'm not. We were walking off the tennis court, and you know, he was there and me and his wife, and he looked at her and then they both looked at me, and under his breath he said, "Jew."

ROB   Alvy, you're a total paranoid.

ALVY   Wh— How am I a paran—? Well, I pick up on those kind o' things. You know, I was having lunch with some guys from NBC, so I said . . . uh, "Did you eat yet or what?" and Tom Christie said,

"No, didchoo?" Not, did you, didchoo eat? Jew? No, not did you eat, but jew eat? Jew. You get it? Jew eat?

ROB   Ah, Max, you, uh . . .

ALVY   Stop calling me Max.

ROB   Why, Max? It's a good name for you. Max, you see conspiracies in everything.

ALVY   No, I don't! You know, I was in a record store. Listen to this —so I know there's this big tall blond crew-cutted guy and he's lookin' at me in a funny way and smiling and he's saying, "Yes, we have a sale this week on Wagner." Wagner, Max, Wagner—so I know what he's really tryin' to tell me very significantly Wagner.

ROB   Right, Max. California, Max.

ALVY   Ah.

ROB   Let's get the hell outta this crazy city—

ALVY   Forget it, Max.

ROB   —we move to sunny L.A. All of show business is out there, Max.

ALVY   No, I cannot. You keep bringing it up, but I don't wanna live in a city where the only cultural advantage is that you can make a right turn on a red light.

ROB   *(Checking his watch)* Right, Max, forget it. Aren't you gonna be late for meeting Annie?

ALVY   I'm gonna meet her in front of the Beekman. I think I have a few minutes left. Right?

EXTERIOR. BEEKMAN THEATER—DAY.

Alvy stands in front of glass doors of theater, the ticket taker behind him just inside the glass doors. The sounds of city traffic, car horns honking, can be heard while he looks around waiting for Annie. A man in a black leather jacket, walking past the theater, stops in front of Alvy. He looks at him, then moves away. He stops a few steps farther and turns around to look at Alvy again. Alvy looks away, then back at the man. The man continues to stare. Alvy scratches his head, looking for Annie and trying not to notice the man. The man, still staring, walks back to Alvy.

IST MAN   Hey, you on television?

ALVY *(Nodding his head)*   No. Yeah, once in a while. You know, like occasionally.

1ST MAN   What's your name?

ALVY *(Clearing his throat)*   You wouldn't know it. It doesn't matter. What's the difference?

1ST MAN   You were on . . . uh, the . . . uh, the Johnny Carson, right?

ALVY   Once in a while, you know. I mean, you know, every now—

1ST MAN   What's your name?
Alvy is getting more and more uneasy as the man talks; more and more people move through the doors of the theater.

ALVY *(Nervously)*   I'm . . . I'm, uh, I'm Robert Redford.

1ST MAN *(Laughing)*   Come on.

ALVY   Alvy Singer. It was nice—nice . . . Thanks very much . . . for everything.
They shake hands and Alvy pats the man's arm. The man in turn looks over his shoulder and motions to another man. All excited now, he points to Alvy and calls out. Alvy looks impatient.

1ST MAN   Hey!

2ND MAN *(Offscreen)*   What?

1ST MAN   This is Alvy Singer!

ALVY   Fellas . . . you know—Jesus! Come on!

1ST MAN *(Overlapping, ignoring Alvy)*   This guy's on television! Alvy Singer, right? Am I right?

ALVY *(Overlapping 1st man)*   Gimme a break, will yuh, gimme a break. Jesus Christ!

1ST MAN *(Still ignoring Alvy's protestations)*   This guy's on television.

ALVY   I need a large polo mallet!

2ND MAN *(Moving into the screen)*   Who's on television?

1ST MAN   This guy, on the Johnny Carson show.

ALVY *(Annoyed)*   Fellas, what is this—a meeting o' the teamsters? You know . . .

2ND MAN *(Also ignoring Alvy)*   What program?

1ST MAN *(Holding out a matchbook)* Can I have your autograph?

ALVY You don't want my autograph.

1ST MAN *(Overlapping Alvy's speech)* Yeah, I do. It's for my girl friend. Make it out to Ralph.

ALVY *(Taking the matchbook and pen and writing)* Your girl friend's name is Ralph?

1ST MAN It's for my brudder. *(To passers-by)* Alvy Singer! Hey! This is Alvy—

2ND MAN *(To Alvy, overlapping 1st man's speech)* You really Alvy Singer, the . . . the TV star?
Nodding his head yes, Alvy shoves 2nd man aside and moves to the curb of the sidewalk. The two men follow, still talking over the traffic noise.

1ST MAN —Singer!

2ND MAN Alvy Singer over here!
A cab moves into the frame and stops by the curb. Alvy moves over to it about to get in.

ALVY *(Overlapping the two men and stuttering)* I-i-i-i-it's all right, fella. *(As Alvy opens the cab door, the two men still behind him, Annie gets out)* Jesus, what'd you do, come by way of the Panama Canal?

ANNIE *(Overlapping Alvy)* All right, all right, I'm in a bad mood, okay?
Annie closes the cab door and she and Alvy move over to the ticket booth of the theater as they continue to talk.

ALVY Bad mood? I'm standing with the cast of *The Godfather*.

ANNIE You're gonna hafta learn to deal with it.

ALVY Deal! I'm dealing with two guys named Cheech!

ANNIE Okay. *(They move into the ticket line, still talking. A billboard next to them reads "INGMAR BERGMAN'S 'FACE TO FACE,' LIV ULL-MANN")* Please, I have a headache, all right?

ALVY Hey, you are in a bad mood. You-you-you must be getting your period.

ANNIE I'm not getting my period. Jesus, every time anything out of the ordinary happens, you think that I'm getting my period!
They move over to the ticket counter, people in front of them buying tickets and walking offscreen.

ALVY (*Gesturing*) A li-little louder. I think one of them may have missed it! (*To the ticket clerk*) H'm, has the picture started yet?

TICKET CLERK It started two minutes ago.

ALVY (*Hitting his hand on the counter*) That's it! Forget it! I—I can't go in.

ANNIE Two minutes, Alvy.

ALVY (*Overlapping Annie*) No, I'm sorry, I can't do it. We-we've blown it already. I—you know, uh, I-I can't go in in the middle.

ANNIE In the middle? (*Alvy nods his head yes and let's out an exasperated sigh*) We'll only miss the titles. They're in Swedish.

ALVY You wanna get coffee for two hours or something? We'll go next—

ANNIE Two hours? No, u-uh, I'm going in. I'm going in.
She moves past the ticket clerk.

ALVY (*Waving to Annie*) Go ahead. Good-bye.
Annie moves back to Alvy and takes his arm.

ANNIE Look, while we're talking we could be inside, you know that?

ALVY (*Watching people with tickets move past them*) Hey, can we not stand here and argue in front of everybody, 'cause I get embarrassed.

ANNIE All right. All right, all right, so whatta you wanna do?

ALVY I don't know now. You—you wanna go to another movie? (*Annie nods her head and shrugs her shoulders disgustedly as Alvy, gesturing with his hand, looks at her*) So let's go see The Sorrow and the Pity.

ANNIE Oh, come on, we've seen it. I'm not in the mood to see a four-hour documentary on Nazis.

ALVY Well, I'm sorry, I-I can't . . . I-I-I've gotta see a picture exactly from the start to the finish, 'cause—'cause I'm anal.

ANNIE (*Laughing now*) H'h, that's a polite word for what you are.

INTERIOR. THEATER LOBBY.

A lined-up crowd of ticket holders waiting to get into the theater, Alvy and Annie among them. A hum of indistinct chatter can be heard through the ensuing scene.

MAN IN LINE (*Loudly to his companion right behind Alvy and Annie*) We saw the Fellini film last Tuesday. It is not one of his best. It lacks a cohesive structure. You know, you get the feeling that he's not absolutely sure what it is he wants to say. 'Course, I've always felt he was essentially a—a technical film maker. Granted, *La Strada* was a great film. Great in its use of negative energy more than anything else. But that simple cohesive core . . .

Alvy, reacting to the man's loud monologue, starts to get annoyed while Annie begins to read her newspaper.

ALVY (*Overlapping the man's speech*) I'm-I'm-I'm gonna have a stroke.

ANNIE (*Reading*) Well, stop listening to him.

MAN IN LINE (*Overlapping Alvy and Annie*) You know, it must need to have had its leading from one thought to another. You know what I'm talking about?

ALVY (*Sighing*) He's screaming his opinions in my ear.

MAN IN LINE Like all that *Juliet of the Spirits* or *Satyricon,* I found it incredibly . . . indulgent. You know, he really is. He's one of the most indulgent film makers. He really is—

ALVY (*Overlapping*) Key word here is "indulgent."

MAN IN LINE (*Overlapping*) —without getting . . . well, let's put it this way . . .

ALVY (*To Annie, who is still reading, overlapping the man in line who is still talking*) What are you depressed about?

ANNIE I missed my therapy. I overslept.

ALVY How can you possibly oversleep?

ANNIE The alarm clock.

ALVY (*Gasping*) You know what a hostile gesture that is to me?

ANNIE I know—because of our sexual problem, right?

ALVY Hey, you . . . everybody on line at the New Yorker has to know our rate of intercourse?

MAN IN LINE It's like Samuel Beckett, you know—I admire the technique but he doesn't . . . he doesn't hit me on a gut level.

ALVY *(To Annie)* I'd like to hit this guy on a gut level.
The man in line continues his speech all the while Alvy and Annie talk.

ANNIE Stop it, Alvy!

ALVY *(Wringing his hands)* Well, he's spitting on my neck! You know, he's spitting on my neck when he talks.

MAN IN LINE And then, the most important thing of all is a comedian's vision.

ANNIE And you know something else? You know, you're so egocentric that if I miss my therapy you can think of it in terms of how it affects you!

MAN IN LINE *(Lighting a cigarette while he talks)* Gal gun-shy is what it is.

ALVY *(Reacting again to the man in line)* Probably on their first date, right?

MAN IN LINE *(Still going on)* It's a narrow view.

ALVY Probably met by answering an ad in the *New York Review of Books.* "Thirtyish academic wishes to meet woman who's interested in Mozart, James Joyce and sodomy." *(He sighs; then to Annie)* Whatta you mean, *our* sexual problem?

ANNIE Oh!

ALVY I-I-I mean, I'm comparatively normal for a guy raised in Brooklyn.

ANNIE Okay, I'm very sorry. *My* sexual problem! Okay, *my* sexual problem! Huh?
The man in front of them turns to look at them, then looks away.

ALVY I never read that. That was—that was Henry James, right? Novel, uh, the sequel to *Turn of the Screw? My Sexual* . . .

MAN IN LINE *(Even louder now)* It's the influence of television. Yeah, now Marshall McLuhan deals with it in terms of it being a—a high, uh, high intensity, you understand? A hot medium . . . as opposed to a . . .

ALVY *(More and more aggravated)* What I wouldn't give for a large sock o' horse manure.

MAN IN LINE   . . . as opposed to a print . . .
Alvy steps forward, waving his hands in frustration, and stands facing the camera.

ALVY *(Sighing and addressing the audience)*   What do you do when you get stuck in a movie line with a guy like this behind you? I mean, it's just maddening!
The man in line moves toward Alvy. Both address the audience now.

MAN IN LINE   Wait a minute, why can't I give my opinion? It's a free country!

ALVY   I mean, d— He can give you— Do you hafta give it so loud? I mean, aren't you ashamed to pontificate like that? And-and the funny part of it is, M-Marshall McLuhan, you don't know anything about Marshall McLuhan's . . . work!

MAN IN LINE *(Overlapping)*   Wait a minute! Really? Really? I happen to teach a class at Columbia called "TV Media and Culture"! So I think that my insights into Mr. McLuhan—well, have a great deal of validity.

ALVY   Oh, do yuh?

MAN IN LINE   Yes.

ALVY   Well, that's funny, because I happen to have Mr. McLuhan right here. So . . . so, here, just let me—I mean, all right. Come over here . . . a second.
Alvy gestures to the camera, which follows him and the man in line to the back of the crowded lobby. He moves over to a large stand-up movie poster and pulls Marshall McLuhan from behind the poster.

MAN IN LINE   Oh.

ALVY *(To McLuhan)*   Tell him.

MCLUHAN *(To the man in line)*   I hear—I heard what you were saying. You—you know nothing of my work. You mean, my whole fallacy is wrong. How you ever got to teach a course in anything is totally amazing.

ALVY *(To the camera)*   Boy, if life were only like this!

INTERIOR. THEATER. A CLOSE-UP OF THE SCREEN SHOWING FACES OF GERMAN SOLDIERS.

Credits appear over the faces of the soldiers:

THE SORROW
AND
THE PITY
© CINEMA 5 LTD., 1972
© MARCEL OPHULS, ANDRE HARRIS, 1969
Chronicle of a French town during
the Occupation

NARRATOR'S VOICE *(Over credits and soldiers)*   June fourteenth, nineteen forty, the German army occupies Paris. All over the country, people are desperate for every available scrap of news.

CUT TO:
INTERIOR. BEDROOM—NIGHT.

Annie is sitting up in bed reading.

ALVY *(Offscreen)*   Boy, those guys in the French Resistance were really brave, you know? Got to listen to Maurice Chevalier sing so much.

ANNIE   M'm, I don't know, sometimes I ask myself how I'd stand up under torture.

ALVY *(Offscreen)*   You? You kiddin'? *(He moves into the frame, lying across the bed to touch Annie, who makes a face)* If the Gestapo would take away your Bloomingdale's charge card, you'd tell 'em everything.

ANNIE   That movie makes me feel guilty.

ALVY   Yeah, 'cause it's supposed to.
He starts kissing Annie's arm. She gets annoyed and continues to read.

ANNIE   Alvy, I . . .

ALVY   What-what-what-what's the matter?

ANNIE   I—you know, I don't wanna.

ALVY *(Overlapping Annie, reacting)*   What-what—I don't . . . It's not natural! We're sleeping in a bed together. You know, it's been a long time.

ANNIE   I know, well, it's just that—you know, I mean, I-I-I-I gotta sing tomorrow night, so I have to rest my voice.

ALVY (*Overlapping Annie again*) It's always some kind of an excuse. It's— You know, you used to think that I was very sexy. What . . . When we first started going out, we had sex constantly . . . We're-we're probably listed in the *Guinness Book of World Records*.

ANNIE (*Patting Alvy's hand solicitously*) I know. Well, Alvy, it'll pass, it'll pass, it's just that I'm going through a phase, that's all.

ALVY M'm.

ANNIE I mean, you've been married before, you know how things can get. You were very hot for Allison at first.

CUT TO:
INTERIOR. BACKSTAGE OF AUDITORIUM—NIGHT.

Allison, clipboard in hand, walks about the wings, stopping to talk to various people. Musicians, performers and technicians mill about, busy with activity. Allison wears a large "ADLAI" button, as do the people around her. The sounds of a comedian on the stage of the auditorium can be heard, occasionally, interrupted by chatter and applause from the offscreen audience. Allison stops to talk to two women; they, too, wear "ADLAI" buttons.

ALLISON (*Looking down at the clipboard*) Ma'am, you're on right after this man . . . about twenty minutes, something like that.

WOMAN Oh, thank you.
Alvy moves into the frame behind Allison. He taps her on the shoulder; she turns to face him.

ALVY (*Coughing*) Excuse . . . excuse me, when do I go on?

ALLISON (*Looking down at the clipboard*) Who are you?

ALVY Alvy . . . Alvy Singer. I'm a comedian.

ALLISON Oh, comedian. Yes. Oh, uh . . . you're on next.

ALVY (*Rubbing his hands together nervously*) What do you mean, next?

ALLISON (*Laughing*) Uh . . . I mean you're on right after this act.

ALVY (*Gesturing*) No, it can't be, because he's a comic.

ALLISON Yes.

ALVY So what are you telling me, you're putting on two comics in a row?

ALLISON   Why not?

ALVY   No, I'm sorry, I'm not goin'—   I can't . . . I don't wanna go on after that comedian.

ALLISON   It's okay.

ALVY   No, because they're—they're laughing, so *(He starts laughing nervously)* I-I-I'd rather not. If you don't mind, I prefer—

ALLISON *(Overlapping)*   Will you relax, please? They're gonna love you, I know.

ALVY *(Overlapping)*   —I prefer not to, because . . . look, they're laughing at him. See, so what are yuh telling me—
They move closer to the stage, looking out from the wings.

ALLISON *(Overlapping)*   Yes.

ALVY *(Overlapping)*   —that I've got to . . . ah . . . ah . . . They're gonna laugh at him for a couple minutes, then I gotta go out there, I gotta . . . get laughs, too. How much can they laugh? *(Offscreen)* They-they-they're laughed out.

ALLISON *(Offscreen)*   Do you feel all right?
As Allison and Alvy look out at the stage, the camera cuts to their point of view: a comedian standing at a podium in front of huge waving pictures of Adlai Stevenson. The audience, laughing and clapping, sits at round tables in clusters around the room.
The camera moves back to Allison and Alvy watching the stage. Alvy is wringing his hands nervously.

COMEDIAN *(Offscreen, onstage)*   You know . . .
Alvy starts looking Allison up and down; people in the background mill about.

ALVY *(Above the chatter around him)*   Look, what's your—what's your name?

COMEDIAN *(Offscreen)*   . . . General Eisenhower is not . . .

ALLISON *(Looking out at the stage)*   Allison.

ALVY   Yeah? Allison what?

ALLISON *(Still looking offscreen)*   Portchnik.

COMEDIAN   . . . a group from the . . .

ALVY *(Over the comedian's voice)* Portchnik . . . that's nice.
He nods his head.

ALLISON Thank you.

ALVY *(In disbelief, almost to himself)* Allison Portchnik . . . ! *(He whistles
and sticks out his tongue offscreen, reacting)* So, uh . . . whatta yuh telling
me, yuh work for the Stevenson all the time, or what?

ALLISON *(Still looking offscreen)* No, no, no, I'm, uh, I'm in the midst
of doing my thesis.

ALVY On what?

ALLISON "On Political Commitment in Twentieth-Century Literature."

ALVY Y-y-you like New York Jewish Left-Wing Liberal Intellectual
Central Park West Brandeis University . . . uh, the Socialist Summer
Camps and the . . . the father with the Ben Shahn drawings, right?
And you really, you know, strike-oriented kind of—uh, stop me
before I make a complete imbecile of myself.

ALLISON No, that was wonderful. I love being reduced to a cultural
stereotype.

ALVY Right, I'm a bigot, you know, but for the left. *(He stands, hands
in pockets, looking out at the stage. The comedian is finished and the audience
is applauding. Allison looks at him as people bustle around them)* Oh, I have
to go out there.
He puts his hands on Allison's shoulders.

ALLISON *(Looking at Alvy)* Yes.
Alvy straightens his tie nervously.

ALVY Say something encouraging quickly.

ALLISON I think you're cute.

ALVY Thank you.

ALLISON *(Laughing)* M'mmm, h'h. Go ahead.
*The crowd applauds. Alvy moves onto the stage as the previous comedian
walks off. The audience continues to applaud as he moves to the podium.
Allison stands in the wings watching, toying with the pencil from her clipboard.*

ALVY *(Coughing)* Thank you. I-I don't know why they would have me at this kind of rally 'cause . . . *(He clears his throat)* Excuse me, I'm not essentially a political comedian at all.
The audience starts to laugh.

ALVY I . . . interestingly had, uh, dated . . . a woman in the Eisenhower Administration . . . briefly . . . and, uh, it was ironic to me 'cause, uh . . . tsch . . . 'cause I was trying to, u-u-uh, do to her what Eisenhower has been doing to the country for the last eight years.
The audience is with him, laughing, as Allison continues to watch offstage.

INTERIOR. APARTMENT BEDROOM.

Allison and Alvy are on the bed, kissing. There are books all over the room; a fireplace, unlit, along one of the walls. Alvy suddenly breaks away and sits on the edge of the bed. Allison looks at him.

ALVY H'm, I'm sorry, I can't go through with this, because it—I can't get it off my mind, Allison . . . it's obsessing me!

ALLISON Well, I'm getting tired of it. I need your attention.
Alvy gets up from the bed and starts walking restlessly around the room, gesturing with his hands.

ALVY It—but it-it . . . doesn't make any sense. He drove past the book depository and the police said conclusively that it was an exit wound. So—how is it possible for Oswald to have fired from two angles at once? It doesn't make sense.

ALLISON Alvy.
Alvy, stopping for a moment at the fireplace mantel, sighs. He then snaps his fingers and starts walking again.

ALVY I'll tell you this! He was not marksman enough to hit a moving target at that range. But . . . *(Clears his throat)* if there was a second assassin . . . it— That's it!
Alvy stops at the music stand with open sheet music on it as Allison gets up from the bed and retrieves a pack of cigarettes from a bookshelf.

ALLISON We've been through this.

ALVY If they-they recovered the shells from that rifle.

ALLISON *(Moving back to the bed and lighting a cigarette)* Okay. All right, so whatta yuh saying, now? That e-e-everybody o-o-on the Warren Commission is in on this conspiracy, right?

ALVY Well, why not?

ALLISON Yeah, Earl Warren?

ALVY *(Moving toward the bed)* Hey . . . honey, I don't know Earl Warren.

ALLISON Lyndon Johnson?

ALVY *(Propping one knee on the bed and gesturing)* L-L-Lyndon Johns— Lyndon Johnson is a politician. You know the ethics those guys have. It's like—uh, a notch underneath child molester.

ALLISON Then everybody's in on the conspiracy?

ALVY *(Nodding his head)* Tsch.

ALLISON The FBI, and the CIA, and J. Edgar Hoover and oil companies and the Pentagon and the men's-room attendant at the White House?
Alvy touches Allison's shoulder, then gets up from the bed and starts walking again.

ALVY I-I-I-I would leave out the men's-room attendant.

ALLISON You're using this conspiracy theory as an excuse to avoid sex with me.

ALVY Oh, my God! *(Then, to the camera)* She's right! Why did I turn off Allison Portchnik? She was—she was beautiful. She was willing. She was real . . . intelligent. *(Sighing)* Is it the old Groucho Marx joke? That—that I-I just don't wanna belong to any club that would have someone like me for a member?

EXTERIOR. BEACH HOUSE—DAY.

Alvy's and Annie's voices are heard over the wind-browned exterior of a beach house in the Hamptons. As they continue to talk, the camera moves inside the house. Alvy is picking up chairs, trying to get at the group of lobsters crawling on the floor. Dishes are stacked up in a drying rack, and bags of groceries sit on the counter. There's a table and chairs near the refrigerator.

ANNIE Alvy, now don't panic. Please.

ALVY Look, I told you it was a . . . mistake to ever bring a live thing in the house.

ANNIE   Stop it! Don't . . . don't do that! There.
The lobsters continue to crawl on the floor. Annie, holding out a wooden paddle, tries to shove them onto it.

ALVY   Well, maybe we should just call the police. Dial nine-one-one, it's the lobster squad.

ANNIE   Come on, Alvy, they're only baby ones, for God's sake.

ALVY   If they're only babies, then you pick 'em up.

ANNIE   Oh, all right. All right! It's all right. Here.
She drops the paddle and picks up one of the lobsters by the tail. Laughing, she shoves it at Alvy who jerks backward, squeamishly.

ALVY   Don't give it to me. Don't!

ANNIE *(Hysterically)*   Oooh! Here! Here!

ALVY *(Pointing)*   Look! Look, one crawled behind the refrigerator. It'll turn up in our bed at night. *(They move over to the refrigerator; Alvy moves as close to the wall as possible as Annie, covering her mouth and laughing hysterically, teasingly dangles a lobster in front of him)* Will you get outta here with that thing? Jesus!

ANNIE *(Laughing, to the lobster)*   Get him!

ALVY *(Laughing)*   Talk to him. You speak shellfish! *(He moves over to the stove and takes the lid off a large steamer filled with boiling water)* Hey, look . . . put it in the pot.

ANNIE *(Laughing)*   I can't! I can't put him in the pot. I can't put a live thing in hot water.

ALVY *(Overlapping)*   Gimme! Gimmee! Let me do it! What—what's he think we're gonna do, take him to the movies?
Annie hands the lobster to Alvy as he takes it very carefully and drops it gingerly into the pot and puts the cover back on.

ANNIE *(Overlapping Alvy and making sounds)*   Oh, God! Here yuh go! Oh, good, now he'll think— *(She screams)* Aaaah! Okay.

ALVY *(Overlapping Annie)*   Okay, it's in. It's definitely in the pot!

ANNIE   All right. All right. All right.
She moves hurriedly across the kitchen and picks up another lobster. Smiling, she places it on the counter as Alvy stands beside the refrigerator trying to push it from the wall.

ALVY Annie, there's a big lobster behind the refrigerator. I can't get it out. This thing's heavy. Maybe if I put a little dish of butter sauce here with a nutcracker, it will run out the other side, you know what I mean?

ANNIE *(Overlapping)* Yeah. I'm gonna get my . . . I'm gonna get my camera.

ALVY You know, I—I think . . . if I could pry this door off . . . We shoulda gotten steaks 'cause they don't have legs. They don't run around.
Annie rushes out of the room to get her camera as Alvy picks up the paddle. Trying to get at the lobsters, he ends up knocking over dishes and hitting the chandelier. Holding the paddle, he finally leans back against the sink. Annie, standing in the doorway, starts taking pictures of him.

ANNIE Great! Great! *(Screaming)* Goddammit! *(Screaming)* Ooooh! These are . . . p-p-p-pick this lobster up. Hold it, please!

ALVY All right! All right! All right! All right! Whatta yuh mean? Are yuh gonna take pictures now?

ANNIE It'll make great— Alvy, be— Alvy, it'll be wonderful . . . Ooooh, lovely!

ALVY *(Picking up the lobster Annie placed on the counter earlier)* All right, here! Oh, God, it's disgusting!
Alvy drops the lobster back down on the counter, sticking out his tongue and making a face.

ANNIE Don't be a jerk. One more, Alvy, please, one more picture. *(Reluctantly Alvy picks up the lobster again as Annie takes another picture)* Oh, oh, good, good!

EXTERIOR. OCEAN FRONT—DUSK.

The camera pans Annie and Alvy as they walk along the shore.

ALVY So, so—well, here's what I wanna know. W-what . . . *(He clears his throat)* Am I your first big romance?

ANNIE Oh . . . no, no, no, no, uh, uh. No.

ALVY Well, then, w-who was?

ANNIE Oh, well, let's see, there was Dennis, from Chippewa Falls High School.

CUT TO:
FLASHBACK OF DENNIS LEANING AGAINST A CAR.

It's night. Behind him is a movie theater with "MARILYN MONROE, 'MISFITS' " on the marquee. He looks at his watch as the younger Annie, in a beehive hairdo, moves into the frame. They kiss quickly and look at each other, smiling.

ALVY'S VOICE *(Offscreen)* Dennis—right, uh, uh . . . local kid probably, would meetcha in front of the movie house on Saturday night.

ANNIE'S VOICE Oh, God, you should've seen what I looked like then.

ALVY'S VOICE *(Offscreen, laughing)* Oh, I can imagine. P-p-probably the wife of an astronaut.

ANNIE'S VOICE Then there was Jerry, the actor.

CUT TO:
FLASHBACK OF BRICK-WALLED APARTMENT—NIGHT.

The younger Annie and Jerry lean against the wall; Jerry is running his hand down Annie's bare arm. Annie and Alvy walk into the room, observing the younger Annie, in jeans and T-shirt, with Jerry.

ALVY'S VOICE *(Laughing)* Look at you, you-you're such a clown.

ANNIE'S VOICE I look pretty.

ALVY'S VOICE Well, yeah, you always look pretty, but that guy with you . . .

JERRY Acting is like an exploration of the soul. I-it's very religious. Uh, like, uh, a kind of liberating consciousness. It's like a visual poem.

ALVY *(Laughing)* Is he kidding with that crap?

YOUNGER ANNIE *(Laughing)* Oh, right. Right, yeah, I think I know exactly what you mean, when you say "religious."

ALVY *(Incredulous, to Annie)* You do?

ANNIE *(Still watching)* Oh, come on—I mean, I was still younger.

ALVY Hey, that was last year.

JERRY It's like when I think of dying. You know how I would like to die?

YOUNGER ANNIE No, how?

JERRY I'd like to get torn apart by wild animals.

ALVY'S VOICE Heavy! Eaten by some squirrels.

ANNIE'S VOICE Hey, listen—I mean, he was a terrific actor, and look at him, he's neat-looking and he was emotional . . . Y—hey, I don't think you like emotion too much.
Jerry stops rubbing the younger Annie's arm and slides down to the floor as she raises her foot toward his chest.

JERRY Touch my heart . . . with your foot.

ALVY'S VOICE I-I may throw up!

CUT BACK TO:
EXTERIOR. BEACH—DUSK.

It's now sunset, the water reflecting the last light. The camera moves over the scene. The offscreen voices of Alvy and Annie are heard as they walk, the camera always one step ahead of them.

ANNIE He was creepy.

ALVY Yeah, I-I think you're pretty lucky I came along.

ANNIE *(Laughing)* Oh, really? Well, la-de-da!

ALVY La-de-da. If I—if anyone had ever told me that I would be taking out a girl who used expressions like "la-de-da" . . .

ANNIE Oh, that's right. That you really like those New York girls.

ALVY Well, no . . . not just, not only.

ANNIE Oh, I'd say so. You married—

CUT TO:
INTERIOR. NEW YORK CITY APARTMENT—NIGHT.

A cocktail party is in progress, the rooms crowded with guests as Alvy and Robin make their way through the people. A waiter, carrying a tray, walks past them. Alvy reaches out to pick up a glass; Robin reaches over and picks it off the tray first. There is much low-key chatter in the background.

ANNIE *(Offscreen)* —two of them.

ROBIN   There's Henry Drucker. He has a chair in history at Princeton. Oh, the short man is Hershel Kaminsky. He has a chair in philosophy at Cornell.

ALVY   Yeah, two more chairs and they got a dining-room set.

ROBIN   Why are you so hostile?

ALVY   *(Sighing)* 'Cause I wanna watch the Knicks on television.

ROBIN   *(Squinting)* Is that Paul Goodman? No. And be nice to the host because he's publishing my book. Hi, Doug! Douglas Wyatt. "A Foul-Rag-and-Bone Shop-of-the-Heart."
They move through the rooms, Robin holding a drink in one hand, her arm draped in Alvy's; the crowd mills around them.

ALVY   *(Taking Robin's hand)*   I'm so tired of spending evenings making fake insights with people who work for *Dysentery.*

ROBIN   *Commentary.*

ALVY   Oh, really, I heard that *Commentary* and *Dissent* had merged and formed *Dysentery.*

ROBIN   No jokes—these are friends, okay?

INTERIOR. BEDROOM.

Alvy sits on the foot of the bed watching the Knicks game on television.

TV ANNOUNCER *(Offscreen)* Cleveland Cavaliers losing to the New York Knicks.
Robin enters the room, slamming the door.

ROBIN Here you are. There's people out there.

ALVY Hey, you wouldn't believe this. Two minutes ago, the Knicks are ahead fourteen points, and now . . . *(Clears his throat)* they're ahead two points.

ROBIN Alvy, what is so fascinating about a group of pituitary cases trying to stuff the ball through a hoop?

ALVY *(Looking at Robin)* What's fascinating is that it's physical. You know, it's one thing about intellectuals, they prove that you can be absolutely brilliant and have no idea what's going on. But on the other hand . . . *(Clears his throat)* the body doesn't lie, as-as we now know.
Alvy reaches over, pulls Robin down onto the bed. He kisses her and moves farther up on the bed.

ROBIN Stop acting out.
She sits on the edge of the bed, looking down at the sprawled-out Alvy.

ALVY No, it'll be great! It'll be great, be-because all those Ph.D.s are in there, you know, like . . . discussing models of alienation and we'll be in here quietly humping.
He pulls Robin toward him, caressing her as she pulls herself away.

ROBIN Alvy, don't! You're using sex to express hostility.

ALVY " 'Why—why do you always r-reduce my animal urges to psychoanalytic categories?' *(Clears his throat)* he said as he removed her brassiere . . ."

ROBIN *(Pulling away again)* There are people out there from *The New Yorker* magazine. My God! What would they think?
She gets up and fixes the zipper on her dress. She turns and moves toward the door.

INTERIOR. APARTMENT—NIGHT.

Robin and Alvy are in bed. The room is in darkness. Outside, a siren starts blaring.

ROBIN   Oh, I'm sorry!

ALVY   Don't get upset!

ROBIN   Dammit! I was so close.
She flips on the overhead lamp and turns on her side. Alvy turns to her.

ALVY   *(Gesturing)*   Jesus, last night it was some guy honking his car horn. I mean, the city can't close down. You know, what-whatta yuh gonna do, h-have 'em shut down the airport, too? No more flights so we can have sex?

ROBIN   *(Reaching over for her eyeglasses on the night table)*   I'm too tense. I need a Valium. My analyst says I should live in the country and not in New York.

ALVY   Well, I can't li—   We can't have this discussion all the time. The country makes me nervous. There's . . . You got crickets and it-it's quiet . . . there's no place to walk after dinner, and . . . uh, there's the screens with the dead moths behind them, and . . . uh, yuh got the-the Manson family possibly, yuh got Dick and Terry—

ROBIN   *(Interrupting)*   Okay, okay, my analyst just thinks I'm too tense. Where's the goddamn Valium?
She fumbles about the floor for the Valium, then back on the bed.

ALVY   Hey, come on, it's quiet now. We can—we can start again.

ROBIN   I can't.

ALVY   What—

ROBIN   My head is throbbing.

ALVY   Oh, you got a headache!

ROBIN   I have a headache.

ALVY   Bad?

ROBIN   Oswald and ghosts.

ALVY   Jesus!
He begins to get out of bed.

ROBIN   Where are you going?

ALVY   Well, I'm-I'm gonna take another in a series of cold showers.

EXTERIOR. MEN'S LOCKER ROOM OF THE TENNIS CLUB.

Rob and Alvy, carrying tennis rackets, come through the door of the locker room to the lobby. They are dressed in tennis whites. They walk toward the indoor court.

ROB Max, my serve is gonna send yuh to the showers—

ALVY Right, right, so g-get back to what we were discussing, the failure of the country to get behind New York City is-is anti-Semitism.

ROB Max, the city is terribly worried.

ALVY But the— I'm not discussing politics or economics. This is foreskin.

ROB No, no, no, Max, that's a very convenient out. Every time some group disagrees with you it's because of anti-Semitism.

ALVY Don't you see? The rest of the country looks upon New York like we're-we're left-wing Communist, Jewish, homosexual, pornographers. I think of us that way, sometimes, and I-I live here.

ROB Max, if we lived in California, we could play outdoors every day, in the sun.

ALVY Sun is bad for yuh. Everything our parents said was good is bad. Sun, milk, red meat, college . . .

INTERIOR. TENNIS COURT.

Annie and Janet, in tennis whites, stand on the court holding tennis rackets and balls. They are chattering and giggling.

ANNIE *(Laughing)* I know, but ooh— Egads, here he comes. Okay. *Rob and Alvy enter the court and walk over to the two women. Rob kisses Janet and makes introduction.*

ROB You know Alvy?

JANET Oh, hi, Alvy.

ANNIE *(To Rob)* How are yuh?

ROB *(To Alvy)* You know Annie?

JANET I'm sorry. This is Annie Hall.

ALVY   Hi.

ANNIE   Hi.
Annie and Alvy shake hands.

JANET *(Laughing)*   Alvy.

ROB *(Eager to begin)*   Who's playing who here?

ALVY   Well, uh . . . you and me against them?

ANNIE *(Overlapping Alvy)*   Well . . . so . . . I can't play too good, you know.

JANET *(Laughing)*   I've had four lessons!
The group, laughing and chatting, divide up—Rob and Annie moving to the other side of the net, Alvy and Janet standing where they are. They start to play mixed doubles, each taking turns and playing well. At one point in the game Annie starts to talk to Rob, then turns and sees a ball heading toward her.

ANNIE *(Hitting the ball back)*   Holy gods!

INTERIOR. LOBBY.

Alvy, dressed, puts things into a gym bag. One knee is on the bench and his back is turned from the entrance. Annie walks toward the entrance door dressed in street clothes and carrying her tennis bag over her shoulder. Seeing Alvy, she stops and turns.

ANNIE   Hi. Hi, hi.

ALVY *(Looking over his shoulder)*   Hi. Oh, hi. Hi.

ANNIE *(Hands clasped in front of her, smiling)*   Well . . . bye.
She laughs and backs up slowly toward the door.

ALVY *(Clearing his throat)*   You-you play . . . very well.

ANNIE   Oh, yeah? So do you. Oh, God, whatta—*(Making sounds and laughing)* whatta dumb thing to say, right? I mean, you say it, "You play well," and right away . . . I have to say well. Oh, oh . . . God, Annie. *(She gestures with her hand)* Well . . . oh, well . . . la-de-da, la-de-da, la-la.
She turns around and moves toward the door.

ALVY *(Still looking over his shoulder)*   Uh . . . you-you wanna lift?

ANNIE *(Turning and aiming her thumb over her shoulder)* Oh, why—uh
. . . y-y-you gotta car?

ALVY No, um . . . I was gonna take a cab.

ANNIE *(Laughing)* Oh, no, I have a car.

ALVY You have a car? *(Annie smiles, hands folded in front of her)* So
. . . *(Clears his throat)* I don't understand why . . . if you have a car,
so then—then wh-why did you say "Do you have a car?" . . . like you
wanted a lift?

ANNIE I don't . . . *(Laughing)* I don't . . . Geez, I don't know, I've
. . . I wa— This . . . yeah, I got this VW out there . . . *(Laughing
and gesturing toward the door)* What a jerk, yeah. Would you like a lift?

ALVY *(Zipping up his bag)* Sure. W-w-w-which way yuh goin'?

ANNIE Me? Oh, downtown!

ALVY Down— I'm-I'm goin' uptown.

ANNIE *(Laughing)* Oh, well, I'm goin' uptown, too.

ALVY Uh, well, you just said you were going downtown.

ANNIE Yeah, well, I'm, but I . . .
*Alvy picks up his bag and moves toward the door. As he turns his bag around,
the handle of the tennis racket hits Annie between the legs.*

ALVY *(Laughing)* So sorry.

ANNIE *(Laughing)* I mean, I can go uptown, too. I live uptown, but
. . . uh, what the hell, I mean, it'd be nice having company, you know
—I mean, I hate driving alone.

ALVY *(Making sounds)* Yeah.
They walk out the door.

EXTERIOR. NEW YORK STREET—DAY.

*Alvy and Annie in the VW as Annie speeds down a city street near the East
River.*

ALVY So, how long do you know Janet? Where do you know her from?

ANNIE *(Laughing)* Oh, I'm in her acting class.

ALVY Oh, you're an actress.

ANNIE   Well, I do commercials, sort of . . .
She zooms down the wrong lane, cars swerving out of her way. A horn blows.

ALVY   I, uh . . . well, you're not from New York, right?

ANNIE   No, Chippewa Falls.

ALVY   Right! *(A pause)* Where?

ANNIE   Wisconsin.

ALVY   *(Finally reacting)*   Uh, you're driving a . . . bit rapidly.

ANNIE   Uh, don't worry, I'm a very—*(A car moves closer to the VW, almost on top of it in the wrong direction. Annie swerves away at the very last minute)*—a very good driver. *(Alvy rubs his head nervously, staring out the window as Annie speeds along)* So, listen—hey, you want some gum, anyway?
Annie looks down beside her, searching for the gum.

ALVY   No, no thanks. Hey, don't—

ANNIE   Well, where is it? I—

ALVY   No, no, no, no, you just . . . just watch the road. I'll get it—

ANNIE   Okay.
They both fumble around in her pocketbook. Alvy looks up to see the entire front of a truck in Annie's windshield. She swerves just in time.

ALVY   —for yuh.

ANNIE   Okay, that's good.
Alvy continues to look for the gum while Annie zooms down the city streets.

ANNIE   All right.

ALVY   I'll getcha a piece.

ANNIE   Yeah . . . so, listen—you drive?

ALVY   Do I drive? Uh, no, I gotta—I gotta problem with driving.

ANNIE   Oh, you do?

ALVY   Yeah. I got, uh, I got a license but I have too much hostility.

ANNIE   Oh, right . . .

ALVY   Nice car.

ANNIE   Huh?

ALVY   You keep it nice. *(He pulls a half-eaten sandwich out of her bag)* Can I ask you, is this—is this a sandwich?

ANNIE   Huh? Oh, yeah.

EXTERIOR. STREET—DAY.

Cars are parked on both sides of the street as the VW rounds the corner.

ANNIE   I live over here. Oh, my God! Look! There's a parking space! *With brakes squealing, Annie turns the VW sharply into the parking spot. Annie and Alvy get out, Alvy looking over his shoulder as he leaves the car.*

ALVY   That's okay, you . . . we-we can walk to the curb from here.

ANNIE   Don't be funny.

ALVY   You want your tennis stuff?

ANNIE   Huh? Oh . . . yeah.

ALVY   You want your gear? Here you go.
Alvy reaches into the back of the car and takes out tennis equipment. He hands her her things. People pass by on the street.

ANNIE   *(Laughing)*   Yeah, thanks. Thanks a lot. Well . . .

ALVY   *(Sighing)*   Well, thanks, thank you. You-you're . . . you're a wonderful tennis player.

ANNIE   *(Laughing)*   Oh.
Alvy shakes hands with Annie.

ALVY   You're the worst driver I've ever seen in my life . . . that's including any place . . . the worst . . . Europe, United . . . any place . . . Asia.

ANNIE   *(Laughing)*   Yeah.

ALVY   And I love what you're wearin'.
Alvy touches the tie Annie is wearing around her neck.

ANNIE   Oh, you do? Yeah? Oh, well, it's uh . . . this is, uh . . . this tie is a present, from Grammy Hall.
Annie flips the bottom of the tie.

ALVY Who? Grammy? Grammy Hall?

ANNIE *(Laughing and nodding her head)* Yeah, my grammy.

ALVY You're jo— Whatta yuh kid— What did you do, grow up in a Norman Rockwell painting?

ANNIE *(Laughing)* Yeah, I know.

ALVY Your grammy!

ANNIE I know, it's pretty silly, isn't it?

ALVY Jesus, my-my grammy . . . n-never gave gifts, you know. She-she was too busy getting raped by Cossacks.

ANNIE *(Laughing)* Well . . .

ALVY Well . . . thank you again.

ANNIE Oh, yeah, yeah.

ALVY I'll see yuh.

ANNIE *(Overlapping, gesturing)* Hey, well, listen . . . hey, you wanna come upstairs and, uh . . . and have a glass of wine and something? Aw, no, I mean . . . I mean, you don't have to, you're probably late and everything else . . .

ALVY No, no, that'll be fine. I don't mind. Sure.

ANNIE You sure?

ALVY *(Overlapping)* No, I got time.

ANNIE Okay.

ALVY Sure, I got . . . I got nothing, uh, nothing till my analyst's appointment.
They move toward Annie's apartment building.

ANNIE Oh, you see an analyst?

ALVY Y-y-yeah, just for fifteen years.

ANNIE Fifteen years?

ALVY Yeah, uh, I'm gonna give him one more year and then I'm goin' to Lourdes.

ANNIE Fifteen—aw, come on, you're . . . yeah, really?

INTERIOR. ANNIE'S APARTMENT.

Alvy, standing, looks around the apartment. There are lots of books, framed photographs on the white wall. A terrace can be seen from the window. He picks up a copy of Ariel, *by Sylvia Plath, as Annie comes out of the kitchen carrying two glasses. She hands them to Alvy.*

ALVY Sylvia Plath.

ANNIE M'hm.

ALVY Interesting poetess whose tragic suicide was misinterpreted as romantic, by the college-girl mentality.

ANNIE Oh, yeah.

ALVY Oh, sorry.

ANNIE Right. Well, I don't know, I mean, uh, some of her poems seem neat, you know.

ALVY Neat?

ANNIE Neat, yeah.

ALVY Uh, I hate to tell yuh, this is nineteen seventy-five, you know that "neat" went out, I would say, at the turn of the century. *(Annie laughs)* Who-who are—who are those photos on the wall?

ANNIE *(Moving over to the photographs)* Oh . . . oh, well, you see now . . . now, uh, that's my dad, that's Father—and that's my . . . brother, Duane.

ALVY Duane?

ANNIE *(Pointing)* Yeah, right, Duane—and over there is Grammy Hall, and that's Sadie.

ALVY Well, who's Sadie?

ANNIE Sadie? Oh, well, Sadie . . . *(Laughing)* Sadie met Grammy through, uh, through Grammy's brother George. Uh, George was real sweet, you know, he had that thing. What is that thing where you, uh, where you, uh, fall asleep in the middle of a sentence, you know—what is it? Uh . . .

ALVY Uh, narcolepsy.

ANNIE Narcolepsy, right, right. Right. So, anyway, so . . . *(Laughing)* George, uh, went to the union, see, to get his free turkey, be-because, uh, the union always gave George this big turkey at Christmastime because he was . . . *(Annie points her fingers to each side of her head, indicating George was a little crazy)* shell-shocked, you know what I mean, in the First World War. *(Laughing hysterically, she opens a cabinet door and takes out a bottle of wine)* Anyway, so, so . . . *(Laughing through the speech)* George is standing in line, oh, just a sec . . . uh, getting his free turkey, but the thing is, he falls asleep and he never wakes up. So, so . . . *(Laughing)* so, he's dead . . . *(Laughing)* he's dead. Yeah.

Oh, dear. Well, terrible, huh, wouldn't you say? I mean, that's pretty unfortunate.
Annie unscrews the bottle of wine, silent now after her speech.

ALVY   Yeah, it's a great story, though, I mean, I . . . I . . . it really made my day. Hey, I think I should get outta here, you know, 'cause I think I'm imposing, you know . . .

ANNIE *(Laughing)*   Oh, really? Oh, well . . . uh, uh, maybe, uh, maybe, we, uh . . .

ALVY   . . . and . . . uh, yeah, uh . . . uh, you know, I-I-I . . .
They move outside to the terrace, Alvy still holding the glasses, Annie the wine. They stand in front of the railing, Annie pouring the wine into the held-out glasses.

ANNIE   Well, I mean, you don't have to, you know.

ALVY   No, I know, but . . . but, you know, I'm all perspired and everything.

ANNIE   Well, didn't you take, uh . . . uh, a shower at the club?

ALVY   Me? No, no, no, 'cause I ne—   I never shower in a public place.

ANNIE *(Laughing)*   Why not?

ALVY   'Cause I don't like to get naked in front of another man, you know—it's, uh . . .

ANNIE *(Laughing)*   Oh, I see, I see.

ALVY   You know, I don't like to show my body to a man of my gender—

ANNIE   Yeah. Oh, yeah. Yeah, I see. I guess—

ALVY   —'cause, uh, you never know what's gonna happen.

ANNIE *(Sipping her wine and laughing)*   Fifteen years, huh?

ALVY   Fifteen years, yeah.

ANNIE   Yeah. Oh, God bless!
They put their glasses together in a toast.

ALVY   God bless.

ANNIE *(Laughing)*   Well, uh . . . *(Pausing)* You're what Grammy Hall would call a real Jew.

ALVY *(Clearing his throat)* Oh, thank you.

ANNIE *(Smiling)* Yeah, well . . . you—She hates Jews. She thinks that they just make money, but let me tell yuh, I mean, she's the one—yeah, is she ever. I'm tellin' yuh.

ALVY *(Pointing toward the apartment after a short pause)* So, did you do those photographs in there or what?

ANNIE *(Nodding, her hand on her hip)* Yeah, yeah, I sorta dabble around, you know.
    (Annie's thoughts pop on the screen as she talks: I dabble? Listen to me—what a jerk)

ALVY They're . . . they're . . . they're wonderful, you know. They have . . . they have, uh . . . a . . . a quality.
    (As do Alvy's: You are a great-looking girl)

ANNIE Well, I-I-I would—I would like to take a serious photography course soon.
    (Again, Annie's thoughts pop on: He probably thinks I'm a yo-yo)

ALVY Photography's interesting, 'cause, you know, it's—it's a new art form, and a, uh, a set of aesthetic criteria have not emerged yet.
    (And Alvy's: I wonder what she looks like naked?)

ANNIE   Aesthetic criteria? You mean, whether it's, uh, good photo or not?
(I'm not smart enough for him. Hang in there)

ALVY   The-the medium enters in as a condition of the art form itself. That's—
(I don't know what I'm saying—she senses I'm shallow)

ANNIE   Well, well, I . . . to me—I . . . I mean, it's-it's-it's all instinctive, you know. I mean, I just try to uh, feel it, you know? I try to get a sense of it and not think about it so much.
(God, I hope he doesn't turn out to be a shmuck *like the others)*

ALVY   Still, still we—   You need a set of aesthetic guide lines to put it in social perspective, I think.
(Christ, I sound like FM radio. Relax)

They're quiet for a moment, holding wine glasses and sipping. The sounds of distant traffic from the street can be heard on the terrace. Annie, laughing, speaks first.

ANNIE   Well, I don't know. I mean, I guess—I guess you must be sorta late, huh?

ALVY   You know, I gotta get there and begin whining soon . . . otherwise I—   Hey . . . well, are you busy Friday night?

ANNIE   Me? Oh, uh . . . *(Laughing)* no.

ALVY *(Putting his hand on his forehead)*   Oh, I'm sorry, wait a minute, I have something. Well, what about Saturday night?

ANNIE *(Nodding)*   Oh . . . nothing. Not—no, no!

ALVY   Oh, you . . . you're very popular, I can see.

ANNIE *(Laughing)*   I know.

ALVY   Gee, boy, what do you have? You have plague?

ANNIE   Well, I mean, I meet a lot of . . . jerks, you know—

ALVY   Yeah, I meet a lotta jerks, too.

ANNIE *(Overlapping)*   —what I mean?

ALVY   I think that's, uh—

ANNIE *(Interrupting)* But I'm thinking about getting some cats, you know, and then they . . . Oh, wait a second—oh, no, no, I mean . . . *(Laughing)* oh, shoot! No, Saturday night I'm gonna—*(Laughing)* I'm gonna sing. Yeah.

ALVY You're gonna sing? Do you sing?

ANNIE Well, no, it isn't—

ALVY *(Overlapping)* No kidding?

ANNIE *(Overlapping)* —this is my first time.

ALVY Oh, really? Where? I'd like to come.

ANNIE *(Laughing)* Oh, no, no, no, no, no!

ALVY No, I'm interested!

ANNIE *(Laughing)* Oh, no—I mean, I'm just a-auditioning sort of at this club. I don't—

ALVY *(Overlapping)* No, so help me—

ANNIE *(Overlapping)* —it's my first time.

ALVY That's okay, 'cause I know exactly what that's like. Listen—

ANNIE *(Interrupting)* Yeah.

ALVY *(Overlapping)* —you're gonna like night clubs, they're really a lotta fun.

INTERIOR. NIGHT CLUB—NIGHT.

Annie stands on center stage with a microphone, a pianist behind her. A bright light is focused on her; the rest of the club is in darkness. There are the typical sounds and movements of a night-club audience: low conversation, curling smoke, breaking glass, microphone hum, moving chairs, waiters clattering trays, a ringing phone as Annie sings "It Had to Be You."

EXTERIOR. CITY STREET—NIGHT.

Alvy and Annie walk quickly down the sidewalk.

ANNIE I was awful. I'm so ashamed! I can't sing.

ALVY Oh, listen, so the audience was a tad restless.

ANNIE Whatta you mean, a tad restless? Oh, my God, I mean, they hated me.

ALVY No, they didn't. You have a wonderful voice.

ANNIE No, I'm gonna quit!

ALVY No, I'm not gonna letcha. You have a great voice.

ANNIE Really, do you think so, really?

ALVY Yeah!

ANNIE Yeah?

ALVY It's terrific.

ANNIE *(Overlapping)* Yeah, you know something? I never even took a lesson, either.
They stop in the middle of the sidewalk. Alvy turns Annie around to face him.

ALVY Hey, listen, listen.

ANNIE What?

ALVY Gimme a kiss.

ANNIE Really?

ALVY Yeah, why not, because we're just gonna go home later, right?

ANNIE Yeah.

ALVY And-and . . . uh, there's gonna be all that tension. You know, we never kissed before and I'll never know when to make the right move or anything. So we'll kiss now we'll get it over with and then we'll go eat. Okay?

ANNIE Oh, all right.

ALVY And we'll digest our food better.

ANNIE Okay.

ALVY Okay?

ANNIE Yeah.
They kiss.

ALVY So now we can digest our food.
They turn and start walking again.

ANNIE We can digest our—

ALVY Okay? Yeah.

INTERIOR. DELI—NIGHT.

Annie and Alvy sit down in a booth. The deli is fairly well lit and crowded. Conversation, plates clattering, can be heard over the dialogue. The waiter comes over to them to take their order.

ALVY *(To the waiter)* I'm gonna have a corned beef.

ANNIE *(To the waiter)* Yeah . . . oh, uh, and I'm gonna have a pastrami on white bread with, uh, mayonnaise and tomatoes and lettuce. *(Alvy involuntarily makes a face as the waiter leaves)* Tsch, so, uh, your second wife left you and, uh, were you depressed about that?

ALVY Nothing that a few mega-vitamins couldn't cure.

ANNIE Oh. And your first wife was Allison?

ALVY My first . . . Yes, she was nice, but you know, uh, it was my fault. I was just . . . I was too crazy.

ANNIE Oh.

INTERIOR. DARKENED BEDROOM—NIGHT.

Alvy and Annie in bed together.

ANNIE   M'm, that was so nice. That was nice.

ALVY   As Balzac said . . .

ANNIE   H'm?

ALVY   . . . "There goes another novel." *(They laugh)* Jesus, you were great.

ANNIE   Oh, yeah?

ALVY   Yeah.

ANNIE   Yeah?

ALVY   Yeah, I'm-I'm-I'm a wreck.

ANNIE   No. *(She turns and looks at Alvy, then laughs)* You're a wreck.

ALVY   Really. I mean it. I-I'll never play the piano again.

ANNIE   *(Lighting a joint and laughing)*   You're really nuts. I don't know, you really thought it was good? Tell me.

ALVY   Good? I was—

ANNIE   *(Overlapping)*   No.

ALVY   No, that was the most fun I've ever had without laughing.

ANNIE   *(Laughing)*   Here, you want some?

ALVY   No, no, I-I-I, uh, I don't use any major hallucinogenics because I took a puff like five years ago at a party and I—

ANNIE   Yeah?

ALVY   —tried to take my pants off over my head . . . *(Annie laughs)* . . . my ear.

ANNIE   Oh, I don't know, I don't really. I don't do it very often, you know, just sort of, er . . . relaxes me at first.

ALVY   M'hm. *(He pushes himself up from the bed and looks down at Annie)* You're not gonna believe this, but—

ANNIE   What? What?

CUT TO:
INTERIOR. BOOKSTORE—DAY.

Annie and Alvy browsing in crowded bookstore. Alvy, carrying two books,
Death and Western Thought *and* The Denial of Death, *moves over to*
where Annie is looking.

ALVY Hey?

ANNIE H'm?

ALVY I-I-I'm gonna buy you these books, I think, because I-I think
you should read them. You know, instead of that cat book.

ANNIE *(Looking at the books Alvy is holding)* That's, uh . . . *(Laughing)*
that's pretty serious stuff there.

ALVY Yeah, 'cause I-I'm, you know, I'm, I'm obsessed with-with, uh,
with death, I think. Big—

ANNIE *(Overlapping)* Yeah?

ALVY —big subject with me, yeah.

ANNIE Yeah?
They move over to the cashier line.

ALVY *(Gesturing)* I've a very pessimistic view of life. You should know
this about me if we're gonna go out, you know. I-I-I feel that life is-is
divided up into the horrible and the miserable.

ANNIE M'hm.

ALVY Those are the two categories . . .

ANNIE M'hm.

ALVY . . . you know, they're— The-the horrible would be like, uh,
I don't know, terminal cases, you know?

ANNIE M'hm.

ALVY And blind people, crippled . . .

ANNIE Yeah.

ALVY I don't—don't know how they get through life. It's amazing to
me.

ANNIE M'hm.

ALVY   You know, and the miserable is everyone else. That's—that's all. So-so when you go through life you should be thankful that you're miserable, because that's— You're very lucky . . . to be . . . *(Overlapping Annie's laughter)* . . . to be miserable.

ANNIE   U-huh.

EXTERIOR. PARK—DAY.

It's a beautiful sunny day in Central Park. People are sitting on benches, others strolling, some walking dogs. One woman stands feeding cooing pigeons. Alvy's and Annie's voices are heard offscreen as they observe the scene before them. An older man and woman walk into view.

ALVY   Look, look at that guy.

ANNIE   M'hm.

ALVY   There's-there's-there's-there's Mr. When-in-the-Pink, Mr. Miami Beach, there, you know? *(Over Annie's laughter)* He's the latest! Just came back from the gin-rummy farm last night . . . He placed third.

ANNIE   *(Laughing)* M'hm. Yeah. Yeah.
The camera shows them sitting side by side relaxed on a bench.

ALVY   *(Watching two men approach, one lighting a cigar)* Look at these guys.

ANNIE   Yeah.

ALVY   Oh, that's hilarious. They're back from Fire Island. They're . . . they're sort of giving it a chance—you know what I mean?

ANNIE   Oh! Italian, right?

ALVY   Yeah, he's the Mafia. Linen Supply Business or Cement and Contract, you know what I mean?

ANNIE   *(Laughing)* Oh, yeah.

ALVY   No, I'm serious. *(Over Annie's laughter)* I just got my mustache wet.

ANNIE   Oh, yeah?

ALVY   *(As another man walks by)* And there's the winner of the Truman Capote look-alike contest.

EXTERIOR. STREET—NIGHT.

Alvy and Annie walk almost in silhouette along the dock, the New York City skyline in the background. Alvy has his arm around Annie and they walk slowly. No one else is around.

ANNIE   You see, like you and I . . .

ALVY   You are extremely sexy.

ANNIE   No, I'm not.

ALVY   Unbelievably sexy. Yes, you are. Because . . . you know what you are? You're-you're polymorphously perverse.

ANNIE   Well, what does—what does that mean? I don't know what that is.

ALVY   Uh . . . uh, you're—you're exceptional in bed because you got —you get pleasure in every part of your body when I touch you.

ANNIE   Ooooh!
They stop walking. Holding Annie's arms, Alvy turns her to face him. The 59th Street Bridge, lit up for the night, is in the background.

ALVY   You know what I mean? Like the tip o' your nose, and if I stroke your teeth or your kneecaps . . . you get excited.

ANNIE   Come on. *(Laughing)* Yeah. You know what? You know, I like you, I really mean it. I really do like you.

ALVY   You— Do you love me?

ANNIE   Do I love you?

ALVY   That's the key question.

ANNIE   Yeah.

ALVY   I know you've only known me a short while.

ANNIE   Well, I certainly . . . I think that's very— Yeah, yeah . . . *(Laughing)* yeah. Do you love me?

ALVY   I—uh, love is, uh, is too weak a word for what—

ANNIE   Yeah.

ALVY   —I . . . I lerve you. *(Over Annie's laughter)* You know I lo-ove you, I-I loff you. *(Over Annie's laughter)* There are two *f*s. I-I have to in-vent— Of course I love you.

ANNIE   Yeah.

ALVY *(Putting his arms around her neck)*   Don't you think I do?

ANNIE   I dunno.
They kiss as a foghorn sounds in the distance.

INTERIOR. ALVY'S APARTMENT.

Alvy, somewhat distraught, is following Annie around his apartment, which is filled with boxes and suitcases, clothes and framed pictures. They both carry cartons.

ALVY   Whatta you mean? You're not gonna give up your own apartment, are you?

ANNIE *(Putting down the carton)*   Of course.

ALVY   Yeah, bu-bu-but why?

ANNIE   Well, I mean, I'm moving in with you, that's why.

ALVY   Yeah, but you-you got a nice apartment.

ANNIE   I have a tiny apartment.

ALVY   Yeah, I know it's small.

ANNIE *(Picking up the suitcases and walking into the bedroom)*   That's right, and it's got bad plumbing and bugs.

ALVY *(Picking up some pictures and following Annie into the bedroom)*   All right, granted, it has bad plumbing and bugs, but you-you say that like it's a negative thing. You know, bugs are-are—uh, entomology is a . . . *(Annie, reacting, tosses the suitcases and some loose clothing onto the bed. She sits down on the edge, looking away. Alvy walks in, pictures and carton in hand, still talking)* . . . rapidly growing field.

ANNIE   You don't want me to live with you?

ALVY   How—   I don't want you to live with me? How—   Whose idea was it?

ANNIE   Mine.

ALVY   Ye-ah. Was it . . . It was yours actually, but, uh, I approved it immediately.

ANNIE   I guess you think that I talked you into something, huh?

ALVY *(Putting pictures on the mantel)* No—what, what . . . ? I . . . we live together, we sleep together, we eat together. Jesus, you don't want it to be like we're married, do yuh?
He moves over to the carton of books on the window seat and reaches in. He starts tossing books offscreen.

ANNIE *(Looking up at Alvy)* How is it any different?

ALVY *(Gesturing)* It's different 'cause you keep your own apartment. *(Holding a book, he starts walking around the room)* Because you know it's there, we don't have to go to it, we don't have to deal with it, but it's like a-a-a free-floating life raft . . . that we know that we're not married.
He tosses the book on the bed and walks back to the window seat.

ANNIE *(Still sitting on the bed)* That little apartment is four hundred dollars a month, Alvy.

ALVY *(Looking at Annie)* That place is four hundred dollars a month?

ANNIE Yes, it is.

ALVY *(Whistling)* It's—it's got bad plumbing and bugs. Jesus, I'll— My accountant will write it off as a tax deduction, I'll pay for it.

ANNIE *(Shaking her head)* You don't think I'm smart enough to be serious about.

ALVY Hey, don't be ridiculous.
Alvy moves over to the bed and sits down next to Annie.

ANNIE Then why are you always pushing me to take those college courses like I was dumb or something?

ALVY *(Putting his hand to his forehead)* 'Cause adult education's a wonderful thing. You meet a lotta interesting professors. You know, it's stimulating.

EXTERIOR. COUNTRY HIGHWAY—DAY.

Annie and Alvy, in Annie's VW, driving to their summerhouse. The camera moves with them as they pass a house with a lighted window, blooming foliage. There is no dialogue, but it is a comfortable quiet. Classical music plays in the background.

CUT TO:
INTERIOR. COUNTRY HOUSE—NIGHT.

Annie, sitting cross-legged on a wooden chest in the bedroom, is browsing through a school catalogue. Alvy lies in bed reading.

ANNIE *(Reading)* Does this sound like a good course? Uh, "Modern American Poetry"? Uh, or, uh—let's see now . . . maybe I should, uh, take "Introduction to the Novel."

ALVY Just don't take any course where they make you read *Beowulf.*

ANNIE What? *(Laughing)* Hey, listen, what-what do you think? Do you think we should, uh, go to that-that party in Southampton tonight? *Alvy leans over and kisses her shoulder.*

ALVY No, don't be silly. What-what do we need other people for? *(He puts his arms around her neck, kissing her, Annie making muffled sounds)* You know, we should—we should just turn out the lights, you know, and play hide and salam or something.

ANNIE *(Laughing)* Well, okay. Well, listen, I'm gonna get a cigarette, okay?

ALVY *(Yelling out to her as she leaves the room)* Yeah, grass, right? The illusion that it will make a white woman more like Billie Holiday.

ANNIE *(Offscreen)* Well, have you ever made love high?

ALVY Me, no. You . . . I-I—you know, if I have grass or alcohol or anything I get unbearably wonderful. I get too, too wonderful for words. You know, I don't—I don't know why you have to, uh, get high every time we make love.

ANNIE *(Moving back into the room and lighting a joint)* It relaxes me.

ALVY Oh, you-you have to be artifically relaxed before we can go to bed?

ANNIE *(Closing the door)* Well, what's the difference, anyway?

ALVY Well, I'll give you a shot of sodium pentothal. You can sleep through it.

ANNIE Oh, come on, look who's talking. You've been seeing a psychiatrist for fifteen years. *(She gets into bed and takes a puff of marijuana)* You should smoke some o' this. You'd be off the couch in no time.

ALVY   Oh, come, you don't need that.
Alvy, sitting down on the bed, moves over to Annie and takes the weed from her.

ANNIE   What are you doing?

ALVY *(Kissing her)*   No, no, no, what . . .   You can once, you can live without it once. Come on.

ANNIE   Oh, no, Alvy, please. Alvy, please. *(Laughing and making sounds)* M'mmm.

ALVY   M'm, wait, I got a great idea. *(He gets up and goes over to the closet, taking out a light bulb. He goes back to the bed and turns out the lamp on the night table)* Hang in there for a second. I got a little-little artifact. A little erotic artifact, that-that I brought up from the city, which I think, uh, is gonna be perfect. *(He turns the lamp back on, having replaced the bulb with the red one from the closet)* I just . . . there . . . There's a little Old New Orleans . . . essence. Now-now we can go about our business here and we can even develop photographs if we want to. There, now there. *(He undresses and crawls into bed, taking Annie in his arms)* M'mmm. M'mmm. Hey, is something wrong?

ANNIE   Uh-uh—why?

ALVY   I don't know. You—   It's like you're—you're removed.

ANNIE   No, I'm fine.
As Annie speaks, her inner self, ghostlike, moves up from the bed and sits down on a chair, watching.

ALVY   Really?

ANNIE   U-huh.

ALVY   I don't know, but you seem sort of distant.

ANNIE   Let's just do it, all right?

ALVY *(Kissing and caressing Annie)*   Is it my imagination or are you just going through the motions?

ANNIE'S SPIRIT   Alvy, do you remember where I put my drawing pad? Because while you two are doing that, I think I'm gonna do some drawing.

ALVY *(Reacting)*   You see, that's what I call removed.

ANNIE   Oh, you have my body.

ALVY   Yeah, but that's not—that's no good. I want the whole thing.

ANNIE   *(Sighing)*   Well, I need grass and so do you.

ALVY   Well, it ruins it for me if you have grass *(Clearing his throat)* because, you know, I'm, like, a comedian—

ANNIE   *(Overlapping)*   M'hm.

ALVY   *(Overlapping)*   —so if I get a laugh from a person who's high, it doesn't count. You know—'cause they're always laughin'.

ANNIE   Were you always funny?

ALVY   Hey, what is this—an interview? We're supposed to be making love.

CUT TO:
INTERIOR. OFFICE.

A typical old-fashioned theatrical agency in a Broadway office building. Autographed 8 1/2 × 11's plaster the sloppy room. The agent, chewing a cigar, sits behind his desk talking to one of his clients, a comedian, who stands with his hands in his pockets. A young Alvy sits stiffly in a chair nearby watching.

AGENT   This guy is naturally funny. I think he can write for you.

COMIC   *(Buttoning his jacket)*   Yeah, yeah. Hey, kid, he tells me you're really good. Well, lemme explain a little bit o' how I work. You know, you can tell right off the bat that I don't look like a funny guy when I come—you know, like some o' the guys that come out. You know, right away *(Gesturing)* they're gonna tell yuh their stories, you're gonna fall down, but I gotta be really talented. Material's gotta be sensational for me 'cause I work, you know, with very, very . . . Come on, I'm kinda classy, you know what I mean? Uh . . . uh . . . lemme explain. For instance, I open with an opening song. A musical start like *(Ad-lib singing)* and I walk out *(Ad-lib singing).* "Place looks wonderful from here and you folks look wonderful from here! *(Singing):*
>   "And seein' you there
>   With a smile on your face
>   Makes me shout
>   This must be the place."
Then I stop right in the middle and then I open with some jokes. Now, that's where I need you, right there. For instance, like I say,

"Hey, I just got back from Canada, you know, they speak a lotta French up there. The only way to remember Jeanne d'Arc means the light's out in the bathroom!" *(He laughs. Seated Alvy looks up smiling)* "Oh, I met a big lumberjack . . ."

ALVY'S VOICE *(To himself)*   Jesus, this guy's pathetic.

COMIC *(Overlapping above speech)*   ". . . big lumberjack . . ."

ALVY'S VOICE *(To himself while the comic continues his routine)*   Look at him mincing around, like he thinks he's real cute. You wanna throw up. If only I had the nerve to do my own jokes. I don't know how much longer I can keep this smile frozen on my face. I'm in the wrong business, I know it.

COMIC *(Overlapping above speech)*   " 'Cherie, come back. I love you. *(Shaking his lips and mimicking)* But, uh, Cheri, what will I do with this, uh?' He says, 'Aw, Marie, sometime you make me so mad.' " *(Laughing)* Oh, they scream at that. Now, write me somethin' like that, will yuh? Kinda French number, can yuh do it? Huh, kid?

INTERIOR. THEATER—NIGHT.

The darkened auditorium is filled with college students applauding and cheering, excited, as Alvy stands on spotlighted stage holding the microphone.

ALVY *(Gesturing)*   W-where am I? I-I keep . . . I have to reorient myself. This is the University of Wisconsin, right? So I'm always . . . I'm tense and . . . uh, when I'm playin' a col— I've a very bad history with colleges. You know, I went to New York University and, uh, tsch, I was thrown out of NYU my freshman year . . . for cheating on my metaphysics final. You know, I looked within the soul of the boy sitting next to me— *(The audience laughs; they're with him)* —and when I was thrown out, my mother, who's an emotionally high-strung woman, locked herself in the bathroom and took an overdose of mah-jongg tiles. *(More applause and laughter)* And, uh, tsch, I was depressed. I was . . . in analysis, I-I, uh, was suicidal; as a matter of fact, uh, I would have killed myself but I was in analysis with a strict Freudian and if you kill yourself . . . they make you pay for the sessions you miss.

INTERIOR. BACKSTAGE OF THEATER.
Students mill around Alvy handing him pens and paper for autographs. Annie is next to him, talking over the chattering fans.

ANNIE   Alvy, you were . . .   Alvy, you were just great. I'm not kidding. It was— You were so neat.

ALVY   C-c-coll—   College audiences are so wonderful.

ANNIE   Yeah. Yeah. And you know something? I think that I'm starting to get more of your references, too.

ALVY   Are yuh?

ANNIE   Yeah.

ALVY   Well, the twelve o'clock show is completely different than the nine.

YOUNG WOMAN *(Interrupting)*   May I have your autograph?

ANNIE *(Overlapping above speech)*   Oh.

ALVY *(To Annie, while autographing)*   You're so sure about it.

ANNIE   Oh, I'm really, uh, looking forward to tomorrow. I mean, you know, I think that it'll be really nice to meet Mother and Father. *They start moving toward the exit, a girl snapping a picture of Alvy with a flash camera as they walk through the crowd.*

ALVY   Yeah, I know, they'll hate me immediately. *(To one of his fans)* Thank you.

ANNIE   No, I don't think so. No, I don't think they're gonna hate you at all. On the contrary, I think—

ALVY   Yeah.

ANNIE   It's Easter. You know, we'll have a nice dinner, we'll sit down and eat. I think they're gonna really like you.

EXTERIOR. ANNIE'S PARENTS' HOME—DAY.

The camera shows a neat two-story house surrounded by a well-manicured green lawn, then cuts to:

INTERIOR. DINING ROOM.

Alvy and the Halls are eating Easter dinner. The sun is pouring through a big picture window, shining on a large, elegantly laid out table. Alvy sits, at one end, rubbing his nose and chewing, the Halls flanking him on either side: Mr. and Mrs. Hall, Grammy, and Annie's brother, Duane.

MOM HALL *(Holding her wine glass)* It's a nice ham this year, Mom.
Grammy Hall takes a sip of her wine and nods.

ANNIE *(Smiling at Duane)* Oh, yeah. Grammy always does such a good
job.

DAD HALL *(Chewing)* A great sauce.

ALVY It is. *(Smacking his lips)* It's dynamite ham.
*Grammy Hall stares down the table at Alvy; a look of utter dislike. Alvy
tries not to notice.*

MOM HALL *(To Dad Hall, smoothing her hair)* We went over to the swap
meet. Annie, Gram and I. Got some nice picture frames.

ANNIE We really had a good time.
*Grammy continues to stare at Alvy; he is now dressed in the long black coat
and hat of the Orthodox Jew, complete with mustache and beard.*

MOM HALL *(Lighting a cigarette and turning to Alvy)* Ann tells us that
you've been seeing a psychiatrist for fifteen years.

ALVY *(Setting down his glass and coughing)* Yes. I'm making excellent
progress. Pretty soon when I lie down on his couch, I won't have
to wear the lobster bib.
*Mom Hall reacts by sipping from her glass and frowning. Grammy continues
to stare.*

DAD HALL Duane and I went out to the boat basin.

DUANE We were caulkin' holes all day.

DAD HALL Yeah. *(Laughing)* Randolph Hunt was drunk, as usual.

MOM HALL Oh, that Randolph Hunt. You remember Randy Hunt, Annie. He was in the choir with you.

ANNIE Oh, yes, yes.
Alvy, leaning his elbow on the table, looks out toward the camera.

ALVY *(To the audience)* I can't believe this family. *(Making chewing sounds)* Annie's mother. She really's beautiful. And they're talkin' swap meets and boat basins, and the old lady at the end of the table *(Pointing to Grammy)* is a classic Jew hater. And, uh, they, they really look American, you know, very healthy and . . . like they never get sick or anything. Nothing like my family. You know, the two are like oil and water.
The screen splits in half: on the right is Alvy's family—his mother, father, aunt and uncle—busily eating at the crowded kitchen table. They eat quickly and interrupt one another loudly. On the left the Halls in their dining room. Both dialogues overlap, juxtaposed.

ALVY'S FATHER Aw, let 'im drop dead! Who needs his business?!

ALVY'S MOTHER His wife has diabetes!

ALVY'S FATHER Di-diabetes? Is that any excuse? Diabetes?

ALVY'S UNCLE The man is fifty years old and doesn't have a substantial job.

ALVY'S AUNT *(Putting more meat on her husband's plate)* Is that a reason to steal from his father?

ALVY'S UNCLE Whatta you talkin' about? You don't know what you're talking about.

ALVY'S AUNT Yes, I know what I'm talking about.

ALVY'S MOTHER *(Interrupting)* George, defend him!

ALVY'S UNCLE *(Over Alvy's father's muttering)* No Moskowitz he had a coronary.

ALVY'S AUNT You don't say.

ALVY'S MOTHER We fast.

MOM HALL Stupid Thelma Poindexter . . . to the Veterans Hospital.

DAD HALL My God, he's the new president of the El Regis. Let me tell you, the man is somethin' else.

MOM HALL That's Jack's wife. We used to make that outta raisins—

ANNIE Oh, yes, that's right. Did you see the new play?

MOM HALL Oh, you remember her, Annie.

ANNIE Yes, I do.
The two families start talking back and forth to one another. The screen is still split.

MOM HALL How do you plan to spend the holidays, Mrs. Singer?

DAD HALL Fast?

ALVY'S FATHER Yeah, no food. You know, we have to atone for our sins.

MOM HALL What sins? I don't understand.

ALVY'S FATHER Tell you the truth, neither do we.

CUT TO:
INTERIOR. DUANE'S BEDROOM—NIGHT.

Duane, sitting on his bed, sees Alvy walking past the open door.

DUANE Alvy.

ALVY *(Walking in)* Oh, hi, Duane, how's it goin'?

DUANE This is my room.

ALVY *(Looking around)* Oh, yeah? *(He clears his throat)* Terrific.

DUANE Can I confess something?
Alvy sighs and sits down, leaning his arm on Duane's dresser. Duane's face is highlighted by a single lamp.

DUANE I tell you this because, as an artist, I think you'll understand. Sometimes when I'm driving . . . on the road at night . . . I see two headlights coming toward me. Fast. I have this sudden impulse to turn the wheel quickly, head-on into the oncoming car. I can anticipate the explosion. The sound of shattering glass. The . . . flames rising out of the flowing gasoline.

ALVY *(Reacting and clearing his throat)* Right. Tsch, well, I have to—I have to go now, Duane, because I-I'm due back on the planet earth. *He slowly gets up and moves toward the door.*

INTERIOR. THE HALLS' LIVING ROOM.

Mom and Dad Hall walk into the living room; Annie is with them.

MOM HALL Now, don't let it be so long, now.

ANNIE No.

DAD HALL And look up Uncle Bill, you promise.

ANNIE Okay. Okay.

MOM HALL Oh, he's adorable, Annie.

ANNIE You think so? Do you really?

MOM HALL We're going to take them to the airport.

DAD HALL Oh, no—Duane can. I haven't finished my drink.

ANNIE Yes, Duane is. I'll be right—

MOM HALL M'mmm.

ANNIE I just have time to get the, uh—
She walks out of the room as Mom and Dad Hall kiss.

EXTERIOR. ROAD—NIGHT.

Duane, behind the wheel, stares straight ahead. It is raining very hard, the windshield wipers are moving quickly. The headlights of another car brightens the interior of Duane's car as the camera shows first Duane, then Annie, then Alvy tensely staring straight ahead.

EXTERIOR. STREET—DAY.

The camera holds on a quiet New York City street; the buildings, brownstones. It's a warm day—people sit on front stoops, window boxes are planted. Annie walks into the frame first, then Alvy, who is walking to her right. They walk quickly, side by side, their voices heard before they move into the frame.

ANNIE *(Offscreen)* You followed me. I can't believe it!

ALVY *(Offscreen)* I didn't follow you!

ANNIE You followed me!

ALVY Why? 'Cause I . . . was walkin' along a block behind you staring at you? That's not following!

ANNIE Well, what is your definition of following?

ALVY *(Gasping)* Following is different. I was spying.

ANNIE Do you realize how paranoid you are?

ALVY Paranoid? I'm looking at you. You got your arms around another guy.

ANNIE That is the worst kind of paranoia.

ALVY Yeah—well, I didn't start out spying. I-I thought I'd surprise yuh. Pick you up after school.

ANNIE Yeah—well, you wanted to keep the relationship flexible, remember? It's your phrase.

ALVY Oh, stop it. But you were having an affair with your college professor. That jerk that teaches that incredible crap course "Contemporary Crisis in Western Man"!

ANNIE   'S—"Existential Motifs in Russian Literature"! You're really close.

ALVY   What's the difference? It's all mental masturbation.

ANNIE *(Stopping for a moment)*   Oh, well, now we're finally getting to a subject you know something about!
She walks away.

ALVY *(Catching up to her)*   Hey, don't knock masturbation! It's sex with someone I love.

ANNIE *(Continuing to walk quickly)*   We're not having an affair. He's married. He just happens to think I'm neat.

ALVY *(Still walking next to her)*   "Neat"! There's that— What are you —twelve years old? That's one o' your Chippewa Falls expressions! "He thinks I'm neat."

ANNIE   Who cares? Who cares?

ALVY   Next thing you know he'll find you keen and peachy, you know? Next thing you know he's got his hand on your ass!
They both stop in the middle of the street.

ANNIE   You've always had hostility toward David ever since I mentioned him!

ALVY   David? You call your teacher David?

ANNIE   It's his name.

ALVY   Well, listen, that's, a nice bi—it's a biblical name. Right? W-What does he call you? Bathsheba?
He walks away.

ANNIE *(Calling after him)*   Alvy! Alvy! You're the one who never wanted to make a real commitment. You don't think I'm smart enough! We had that argument just last month, or don't you remember that day?

CUT TO:
INTERIOR. KITCHEN.

Alvy is at the sink washing dishes as the screen cuts to the scene of last month's argument. Annie's voice is heard.

ANNIE *(Offscreen)*   I'm home!

ALVY *(Turning)* Oh, yeah? How'd it go?

ANNIE *(Comes into the kitchen and puts down a bag of groceries on the kitchen table)* Oh, it was . . . *(Laughing)* really weird. But she's a very nice woman.

ALVY Yeah?

ANNIE And I didn't have to lie down on the couch, Alvy, she had me sitting up. So I told her about—about the-the family and about my feelings toward men and about my relationship with my brother.

ALVY M'm.

ANNIE And then she mentioned penis envy . . . Did you know about that?

ALVY Me? I'm—I'm one of the few males who suffers from that, so, so . . . you know.

ANNIE M'hm.

ALVY G-go on, I'm interested.

ANNIE Well, she said that I was very guilty about my impulses toward marriage, and-and children.

ALVY M'hm.

ANNIE And then I remembered when I was a kid how I accidentally saw my parents making love.

ALVY Tsch. Rea— All this happened in the first hour?

ANNIE M'hm.

ALVY That's amazing. I-I-I . . . I've been goin' for fifteen years, I—you know, I don't got . . . nothing like that in—

ANNIE Oh, I told her my dream and then I cried.

ALVY You cried? I've never once cried. Fantastic . . .

ANNIE *(Taking groceries from the bag)* Yeah.

ALVY I whine. I-I-I sit and I whine.

ANNIE In-in . . . Alvy, in my dream Frank Sinatra is holding his pillow across my face and I can't breathe.

ALVY Sinatra?

ANNIE   Yeah, and he's strangling me . . .

ALVY   Yeah?

ANNIE   . . . and I keep, you know, it's—

ALVY   *(Taking a bottle of juice and some celery from the bag)*   Well, well, sure . . . because he's a singer and you're a singer, you know, so it's perfect. So you're trying to suffocate yourself. It-it makes perfect sense. Uh, uh, that's a perfect analytic . . . kind of insight.

ANNIE   *(Pointing her finger at Alvy)*   She said, your name was Alvy Singer.

ALVY   *(Turning to Annie)*   Whatta you mean? Me?

ANNIE   Yeah, yeah, yeah, you. Because in the dream . . . I break Sinatra's glasses.

ALVY   *(Putting his hand to his mouth)*   Sinatra had gl—   You never said Sinatra had glasses. So whatta you saying that I-I'm suffocating you?

ANNIE   *(Turning, a jar in her hand)*   Oh, and God, Alvy, I did . . . this really terrible thing to him. Because then when he sang it was in this real high-pitched voice.

ALVY   *(Thinking)*   Tsch, what'd the doctor say?

ANNIE   *(Putting away some groceries)*   Well, she said that I should probably come five times a week. And you know something? I don't think I mind analysis at all. The only question is, Will it change my wife?

ALVY   Will it change your wife?

ANNIE   Will it change my life?

ALVY   Yeah, but you said, "Will it change my wife"!

ANNIE   No, I didn't. *(Laughing)* I said, "Will it change my life," Alvy.

ALVY   You said, "Will it change . . ." Wife. Will it change . . .

ANNIE   *(Yelling out, angry)* Life. I said, "life."
Alvy turns toward the camera.

ALVY   *(To the audience)*   She said, "Will it change my wife." You heard that because you were there so I'm not crazy.

ANNIE   And, Alvy . . . and then I told her about how I didn't think you'd ever really take me seriously, because you don't think that I'm smart enough.
She walks out of the room.

ALVY *(To Annie's back, gesturing)*   Why do you always bring that up? Because I encourage you to take adult-education courses? I think it's a wonderful thing. You meet wonderful, interesting professors.

CUT TO:
EXTERIOR. STREET.

Annie stands at the open door of a cab, Alvy next to her gesturing as people and cars move by.

ALVY   Adult education is such junk! The professors are so phony. How can you do it?

ANNIE   I don't care what you say about David, he's a perfectly fine teacher!

ALVY *(Interrupting)*   David! David! I can't believe this!

ANNIE   And what are you doing following me around for, anyway?

ALVY   I'm following you and David, if you—

ANNIE *(Interrupting)*   I just think we oughta call this relationship quits!
Annie gets into the cab; Alvy leans over and closes the door.

ALVY   That's fine. That's fine. That's great! *(He turns toward the camera as the cab drives away)* Well, I don't know what I did wrong. *(Gesturing)* I mean, I can't believe this. Somewhere she cooled off to me! *(He walks up to an older woman walking down the street carrying groceries)* Is it—is it something that I did?

WOMAN ON THE STREET   Never something you do. That's how people are. Love fades.
She moves on down the street.

ALVY *(Scratching his head)*   Love fades. God, that's a depressing thought. I-I-I-I have to ask you a question. *(He stops another passer-by, a man)* Don't go any further. Now, with your wife in bed, d-d-does she need some kind o' artificial stimulation like-like marijuana?

MAN ON THE STREET   We use a large vibrating egg.
He walks on.

ALVY (*Continuing to walk*) Large vibrating egg. Well, I ask a psycho-path, I get that kind of an answer. Jesus, I-I, uh, here . . . (*He moves up the sidewalk to a young trendy-looking couple, arms wrapped around each other*) You-you look like a really happy couple. Uh, uh . . . are you?

YOUNG WOMAN Yeah.

ALVY Yeah! So . . . so h-h-how do you account for it?

YOUNG WOMAN Uh, I'm very shallow and empty and I have no ideas and nothing interesting to say.

YOUNG MAN And I'm exactly the same way.

ALVY I see. Well, that's very interesting. So you've managed to work out something, huh?

YOUNG MAN Right.

YOUNG WOMAN Yeah.

ALVY Oh, well, thanks very much for talking to me.
He continues to walk past some other passers-by and moves into the street. A mounted policeman comes by and stops near him. Alvy looks at the horse, as if to speak.

ALVY'S VOICE-OVER You know, even as a kid I always went for the wrong women. I think that's my problem. When my mother took me to see *Snow White*, everyone fell in love with Snow White. I immediately fell for the Wicked Queen.
The scene dissolves into a sequence from the animated Snow White and the Seven Dwarfs. *The Wicked Queen, resembling Annie, sits in the palace before her mirror. Alvy, as a cartoon figure, sits beside her, arms crossed in front of him.*

WICKED QUEEN We never have any fun anymore.

CARTOON FIGURE ALVY How can you say that?

WICKED QUEEN Why not? You're always leaning on me to improve myself.

CARTOON FIGURE ALVY You're just upset. You must be getting your period.

WICKED QUEEN I don't get a period! I'm a cartoon character. Can't I be upset once in a while?
Rob, as a cartoon figure, enters and sits down on the other side of the Wicked Queen.

CARTOON FIGURE ROB   Max, will you forget about Annie? I know lots of women you can date.

CARTOON FIGURE ALVY   I don't wanna go out with any other women.

CARTOON FIGURE ROB   Max, have I got a girl for you. You are going to love her. She's a reporter—
The cartoon figures of Alvy and Rob walk past the Wicked Queen; the screen dissolves into the interior of a concert hall. Rob's voice carries over from the cartoon scene as the screen shows Alvy with the female reporter. It's very crowded, noisy; policeman and reporters are everywhere. Alvy stands with his hands in his pockets, watching the commotion.

CARTOON FIGURE ROB'S VOICE-OVER   —for *Rolling Stone.*

FEMALE REPORTER   I think there are more people here to see the Maharishi than there were to see the Dylan concert. I covered the Dylan concert . . . which gave me chills. Especially when he sang "She takes just like a woman And she makes love just like a woman Yes, she does And she aches just like a woman But she breaks just like a little girl." *(They move toward the aisles as a guard holds up his hands to stop them)* Up to that I guess the most charismatic event I covered was Mick's Birthday when the Stones played Madison Square Garden.

ALVY *(Laughing)*   Man, that's great. That's just great.

REPORTER   You catch Dylan?

ALVY *(Coughing)*   Me? No, no. I-I couldn't make it that ni— My-my raccoon had hepatitis.

REPORTER   You have a raccoon?

ALVY *(Gesturing)*   Tsch, a few.

REPORTER   The only word for this is trans-plendid. It's trans-plendid.

ALVY   I can think of another word.

REPORTER   He's God! I mean, this man is God! He's got millions of followers who would crawl all the way across the world just to touch the hem of his garment.

ALVY   Really? It must be a tremendous hem.

REPORTER   I'm a Rosicrucian myself.

ALVY Are you?

REPORTER Yeah.

ALVY I can't get with any religion that advertises in *Popular Mechanics*. Look— *(The Maharishi, a small, chunky man, walks out of the men's room, huge bodyguards flanking him while policemen hold back the crowds)*— there's God coming outta the men's room.

REPORTER It's unbelievably trans-plendid! I was at the Stones concert in Altamount when they killed that guy, remember?

ALVY Yeah, were yuh? I was—I was at an Alice Cooper thing where six people were rushed to the hospital with bad vibes.

INTERIOR. ALVY'S BEDROOM—NIGHT.

The reporter is sitting up in bed, lighted cigarette in her hand. Alvy, lying next to her, rubs his eyes and puts on his eyeglasses.

REPORTER *(Looking down at herself)* I hope you don't mind that I took so long to finish.

ALVY *(Sighing)* Oh, no, no, don't be . . . tsch . . . don't be silly. You know, *(Yawning)* I'm startin' t'—I'm startin' to get some feeling back in my jaw now.

REPORTER Oh, sex with you is really a Kafkaesque experience.

ALVY Oh, tsch, thank you. H'm.

REPORTER I mean that as a compliment.

ALVY *(Making sounds)* I think—I think there's too much burden placed on the orgasm, you know, to make up for empty areas in life.

REPORTER Who said that?

ALVY *(Rubbing his chin and shoulder)* Uh, oh, I don't know. It might have been Leopold and Loeb. *(The telephone rings. Alvy picks it up, rising up slightly from the bed, concerned, as he talks)* Hello . . . Oh, hi . . . Uh, no, what—what's the matter? What-what-what . . . You sound terrible . . . No, what— Sure I— Whatta yuh—what kind of an emergency? . . . No, well, stay there. Stay there, I'll come over right now. I'll come over right now. Just stay there, I'll come right over.

He hangs up. The reporter sits in bed still, taking in the situation.

INTERIOR. ANNIE'S APARTMENT. HALLWAY.

Annie, looking slightly distraught, goes to open the door to Alvy's knock.

ALVY What's— It's me, open up.

ANNIE *(Opening the door)* Oh.

ALVY Are you okay? What's the matter? *(They look at each other, Annie sighing)* Are you all right? What—

ANNIE There's a spider in the bathroom.

ALVY *(Reacting)* What?

ANNIE There's a big black spider in the bathroom.

ALVY That's what you got me here for at three o'clock in the morning, 'cause there's a spider in the bathroom?

ANNIE My God, I mean, you know how I am about insects—

ALVY *(Interrupting, sighing)* Oooh.

ANNIE —I can't sleep with a live thing crawling around in the bathroom.

ALVY Kill it! For Go— What's wrong with you? Don't you have a can of Raid in the house?

ANNIE *(Shaking her head)* No.
Alvy, disgusted, starts waving his hands and starts to move into the living room.

ALVY *(Sighing)* I told you a thousand times you should always keep, uh, a lotta insect spray. You never know who's gonna crawl over.

ANNIE *(Following him)* I know, I know, and a first-aid kit and a fire extinguisher.

ALVY Jesus. All right, gimme a magazine. I— 'cause I'm a little tired. *(While Annie goes off to find him a magazine, Alvy, still talking, glances around the apartment. He notices a small book on a cabinet and picks it up.)* You know, you, you joke with—about me, you make fun of me, but I'm prepared for anything. An emergency, a tidal wave, an earthquake. Hey, what is this? What? Did you go to a rock concert?

ANNIE Yeah.

ALVY   Oh, yeah, really? Really? How-how'd you like it? Was it—was it, I mean, did it . . . was it heavy? Did it achieve total heavy-ocity? Or was it, uh . . .

ANNIE   It was just great!

ALVY   *(Thumbing through the book)*   Oh, humdinger. When—   Well, I got a wonderful idea. Why don'tcha get the guy who took you to the rock concert, we'll call him and he can come over and kill the spider. You know, it's a—
He tosses the book down on the cabinet.

ANNIE   I called you; you wanna help me . . . or not? H'h? Here.
She hands him a magazine.

ALVY   *(Looking down at the magazine)*   What is this? What are you— Since when do you read the *National Review*? What are you turning into?

ANNIE   *(Turning to a nearby chair for some gum in her pocketbook)*   Well, I like to try to get all points of view.

ALVY   It's wonderful. Then why don'tcha get William F. Buckley to kill the spider?

ANNIE *(Spinning around to face him)* Alvy, you're a little hostile, you know that? Not only that, you look thin and tired.
She puts a piece of gum in her mouth.

ALVY Well, I was in be— It's three o'clock in the morning. You, uh, you got me outta bed, I ran over here, I couldn't get a taxi cab. You said it was an emergency, and I didn't ge— I ran up the stairs. Bel — I was a lot more attractive when the evening began. Look, uh, tell— Whatta you— Are you going with a right-wing rock-and-roll star? Is that possible?

ANNIE *(Sitting down on a chair arm and looking up at Alvy)* Would you like a glass of chocolate milk?

ALVY Hey, what am I—your son? Whatta you mean? I-I came over t'—

ANNIE *(Touching his chest with her hand)* I got the good chocolate, Alvy.

ALVY Yeah, where is the spider?

ANNIE It really is lovely. It's in the bathroom.

ALVY Is he in the bathroom?

ANNIE *(Rising from chair)* Hey, don't squish it, and after it's dead, flush it down the toilet, okay? And flush it a couple o' times.

ALVY *(Moving down the hallway to the bathroom)* Darling, darling, I've been killing spiders since I was thirty, okay?

ANNIE *(Upset, hands on her neck)* Oh. What?

ALVY *(Coming back into the living room)* Very big spider.

ANNIE Yeah?

ALVY Two . . . Yeah. Lotta, lotta trouble. There's two of 'em.
Alvy starts walking down the hall again, Annie following.

ANNIE Two?

ALVY *(Opening a closet door)* Yep. I didn't think it was that big, but it's a major spider. You got a broom or something with a—

ANNIE Oh, I-I left it at your house.

ALVY *(Overlapping)* —snow shovel or anything or something.

ANNIE *(Overlapping)* I think I left it there, I'm sorry.
Reaching up into the closet, Alvy takes out a covered tennis racquet.

ALVY *(Holding the racquet)* Okay, let me have this.

ANNIE Well, what are you doing . . . what are you doing with—

ALVY Honey, there's a spider in your bathroom the size of a Buick.
He walks into the bathroom, Annie looking after him.

ANNIE Well, okay. Oooh.
Alvy stands in the middle of the bathroom, tennis racquet in one hand, rolled magazine in the other. He looks over at the shelf above the sink and picks up a small container. He holds it out, shouting offscreen to Annie.

ALVY Hey, what is this? You got black soap?

ANNIE *(Offscreen)* It's for my complexion.

ALVY Whatta—whatta yuh joining a minstrel show? Geez. *(Alvy turns and starts swapping the racquet over the shelf, knocking down articles and breaking glass)* Don't worry! *(He continues to swat the racquet all over the bathroom. He finally moves out of the room, hands close to his body. He walks into the other room, where Annie is sitting in a corner of her bed leaning against the wall)* I did it! I killed them both. What-what's the matter? Whatta you— *(Annie is sobbing, her hand over her face)*—whatta you sad about? You— What'd you want me to do? Capture 'em and rehabilitate 'em?

ANNIE *(Sobbing and taking Alvy's arm)* Oh, don't go, okay? Please.

ALVY *(Sitting down next to her)* Whatta you mean, don't go? Whatta-whatta-what's the matter? Whatta you expecting—termites? What's the matter?

ANNIE *(Sobbing)* Oh, uh, I don't know. I miss you. Tsch.
She beats her fist on the bed. Reacting, Alvy puts his arm around her shoulder and leans back against the wall.

ALVY Oh, Jesus, really?

ANNIE *(Leaning on his shoulder)* Oh, yeah. Oh. *(They kiss)* Oh! Alvy?

ALVY What?
He touches her face gently as she wipes tears from her face.

ANNIE Was there somebody in your room when I called you?

ALVY W-w-whatta you mean?

ANNIE   I mean was there another—   I thought I heard a voice.

ALVY   Oh, I had the radio on.

ANNIE   Yeah?

ALVY   I'm sorry. I had the television set . . . I had the television—

ANNIE   Yeah.
Alvy pulls her to him and they kiss again.

CUT TO:
INTERIOR—ALVY'S BED.

Alvy is lying in bed next to Annie, who is leaning on her elbow looking down at him. He rubs her arms and she smiles.

ANNIE   Alvy, let's never break up again. I don't wanna be apart.

ALVY   Oh, no, no, I think we're both much too mature for something like that.

ANNIE   Living together hasn't been so bad, has it?

ALVY   It's all right for me, it's been terrific, you know? Better than either one of my marriages. See, 'cause . . . 'cause there's just something different about you. I don't know what it is, but it's great.

ANNIE *(Snickering)*   You know I think that if you let me, maybe I could help you have more fun, you know? I mean, I know it's hard and . . .   Yeah.

ALVY   I don't know.

ANNIE   Alvy, what about . . . what if we go away this weekend, and we could—

ALVY   Tsch, why don't we get . . . why don't we get Rob, and the three of us'll drive into Brooklyn, you know, and we show you the old neighborhood.

ANNIE   Okay, okay. Okay.

ALVY   That'd be fun for yuh. Don't you think—

ANNIE   Yeah.
Alvy raises up his head and they kiss.

EXTERIOR. HIGHWAY.

Annie is behind the wheel in her VW, Rob is beside her, Alvy in the back seat leaning forward so that his head is between them. They're driving down the highway.

ANNIE   —me, my God, it's a great day!

ALVY *(Interrupting)*   Hey, can yuh watch the road? Watch the—

ROB *(Overlapping)*   Yeah, watch the road!

ALVY   You'll total the whole car.

ANNIE *(Laughing)*   Hey, you know, I never even visited Brooklyn before.

ROB   I can't wait to see the old neighborhood.

ALVY   Yeah, the neighborhood's gonna be great.

ROB   We can show her the schoolyard.

ALVY   Right. I was a great athlete. Tell her, Max, I was the best, I was all schoolyard.

ROB   Yes, I remember. *(Annie laughs)* He was all schoolyard. They threw him a football once, he tried to dribble it.

ALVY   Yeah, well, I used to lose my glasses a lot.

EXTERIOR. AMUSEMENT PARK.

Alvy, Annie and Rob move toward the roller coaster on the screen. The area's deserted. Sea gulls are heard.

ALVY   Oh, look, look, there's that . . . that's—that's my old house. That's where I used to live.

ANNIE *(Laughing)*   Holy cow!

ROB   You're lucky, Max—where I used to live is now a pornographic equipment store.
Annie laughs.

ALVY   I have some very good memories there.

ROB   What kind of good memories, Max? Your mother and father fighting all the time.

ALVY   Yeah, and always over the most ridiculous things.

FLASHBACK—INTERIOR. ALVY'S HOUSE.

Alvy's father sits in his chair. His mother is polishing a door while young Alvy lies on the floor playing. Annie, adult Alvy and Rob quietly walk into the scene to watch.

ALVY'S FATHER   You fired the cleaning woman?

ALVY'S MOTHER   She was stealing.

ALVY'S FATHER   But she's colored.

ALVY'S MOTHER   So?

ALVY'S FATHER   So the colored have enough trouble.

ALVY'S MOTHER   She was going through my pocketbook!

ALVY'S FATHER   They're persecuted enough!

ALVY'S MOTHER   Who's persecuting? She stole!
Alvy's father gets up and gets his hard hat. He sits back down and starts polishing it.

ALVY'S FATHER   All right—so we can afford it.

ALVY'S MOTHER   How can we afford it? On your pay? What if she steals more?

ALVY'S FATHER   She's a colored woman, from Harlem! She has no money! She's got a right to steal from us! After all, who is she gonna steal from if not us?

ADULT ALVY *(Yelling into the scene)*   You're both crazy!

ROB   They can't hear you, Max.

ALVY'S MOTHER   Leo . . . I married a fool!

ROB *(Pointing)*   Hey, Max! Who's that?
As the three friends watch Alvy's old living room, the scene has suddenly shifted. A huge crowd stands around the room, laughing, eating, chatting and vibrating with the turns of the roller-coaster ride.

ALVY   It-it-it's the welcome-home party in nineteen forty-five, for my cousin Herbie.

ADULT ALVY *(Pointing)*   Look, look, there's—there's that one over there, that's Joey Nichols, he was my—*(Young Alvy stands next to Joey Nichols, who's sitting in one of the easy chairs. They smile at each other; people and noise all around)*—father's friend. He was always bothering me when I was a kid.

JOEY   Joey Nichols. *(Laughing)* See, Nichols. See, Nichols! *(Joey shows young Alvy his cuff links and tie pin, which are made from nickels, as Alvy stands with hands on hips, unconcerned. Joey then slaps his hand to his forehead and puts a nickel on his forehead)* Yuh see, nickels! You can always remember my name, just think of Joey Five Cents. *(Laughing)* That's me. Joey Five Cents!
Joey grabs Alvy's cheeks and pinches them.

YOUNG ALVY *(Turning away)*   What an asshole!
A group of women stands near a buffet table eating and listening to Alvy's mother and her sister, Tessie, and a young girl, as the three friends watch.

ADULT ALVY   The one who killed me the most was my mother's sister, Tessie.

ALVY'S MOTHER   I was always the sister with good common sense. But Tessie was always the one with personality. When she was younger, they all wanted to marry Tessie.
She touches Tessie's shoulder. Tessie starts to laugh.

ADULT ALVY *(Pointing, to Rob)*   Do you believe that, Max? Tessie Moskowitz had the personality. She's the life of the ghetto, no doubt.

ALVY'S MOTHER *(To the young girl)* She was once a great beauty.
Tessie nods her head "yes."

ROB Tessie, they say you were the sister with personality.

TESSIE *(Addressing the young girl)* I was a great beauty.

ROB Uh, how did this personality come about?

TESSIE *(Grabbing the young girl's cheek)* I was very charming.

ROB There were many men interested in you?

TESSIE *(To the young girl)* Oh, I was quite a lively dancer.
Tessie gyrates back and forth imitating a dancer while Annie and the adult Alvy lean on each other laughing.

ROB *(Laughing)* That's pretty hard to believe.

EXTERIOR. STREET.

Alvy and Annie walk contentedly down a street; Alvy's arm is draped around Annie. People walk by them on the street as they move toward their apartment building.

ANNIE Well, I had a really good day, you know that? It was just a real fine way to spend my birthday.

ALVY Ah? Oh, well, your birthday's not till tomorrow, honey, I hate to tell yuh.

ANNIE Yeah, but it's real close.

ALVY Yeah, but no presents till midnight.

ANNIE *(Laughing)* Oh, darn it.

INTERIOR. APARTMENT.

Annie and Alvy sit on the sofa. Annie's unwrapping a gift while Alvy watches.

ANNIE *(Making sounds)* This is—*(Making sounds)*Huh?
She pulls out flimsy black lingerie from the box.

ALVY Happy birthday.

ANNIE What is this? Is this a . . . present? *(Laughing)* Are you kidding?

ALVY Yeah, hey, why don't yuh try it on?

ANNIE Uh, yeah, uh . . . t-t-this is more like a present for you, yeah, but it's—

ALVY Try it . . . it'll add years to our sex life.

ANNIE *(Looking up at Alvy and laughing)* Uh huh. Yeah. Forget it.
Alvy leans over and hands her another box as she puts down the lingerie.

ALVY Here's a real present.

ANNIE *(Opening the gift)* What . . . oh, yeah? What is this, anyway, huh?

ALVY Check it out.

ANNIE Let me see. Okay, let's . . . oooh, God! *(She takes out a watch from the box)* Oh, you knew I wanted this . . . *(Laughing)* God, it's terrific, God!

ALVY *(Making sounds)* Yeah, I know. Just-just put on the watch, and-and . . . that thing, and we'll just . . .

ANNIE *(Laughing)* Oh! My God! *(Making sounds)*
Alvy kisses Annie.

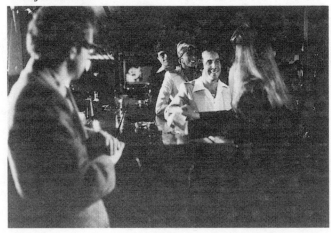

INTERIOR. NIGHT CLUB.

Annie, spotlighted onstage, stands in front of the microphone, smiling. She looks downward and sings "Seems Like Old Times." The audience applauds loudly as the music fades out.

ANNIE *(Laughing)* Thank you.
Alvy sits at the bar, clapping and staring at Annie as she walks over to him and sits down. The low murmur of the night club is surrounding them.

ALVY *(Reacting)* You were—you were sensational. I mean, I—you know, I-I told yuh that if yuh stuck to it, you would be great, and-and, you know, I-I—you-you were sensational.

ANNIE *(Looking at Alvy, smiling)* Yeah, well, we have the, I mean, they were just a terrific audience, I mean, you know, it makes it really easy for me, because I can be . . . huh?
Tony, a famous record personality, pushes through the crowd, moving toward Alvy and Annie. An entourage follows him as he makes his way to their table.

TONY Excuse me.
He shakes hands with Annie, smiling.

ANNIE Oh.

TONY Hi, I'm—I'm Tony Lacey.

ANNIE Well, hi!

TONY Uh, we just wanted to stop by and say that we really enjoyed your sets.

ANNIE *(Laughing)* Oh, yeah, really, oh!

TONY I though it was . . . very musical, and I—I liked it a lot.

ANNIE Oh, neat . . . oh, that's very nice, gosh, thanks a lot.

TONY Are you . . . are you recording? Or do— Are you with any label now?

ANNIE Me? *(Laughing)* No, no, no, not at all.

TONY Uh, well, I'd like to talk to you about that sometime, if you get a chance.
Seated Alvy looks the other way, reacting.

ANNIE Oh. What about?

TONY . . . of possibly working together.

ANNIE *(Looking for the first time at Alvy)* Well, hey, that's, that's nice. Uh. Oh, listen, this is, uh, Alvy Singer. Do you know Alvy? Uh . . . and . . . uh . . . Tony Lacey.

TONY No, I don't—I don't know, but I-I know your work. I'm a big fan of yours.
Tony reaches over and shakes hands with Alvy. The night-club crowd surrounds them all with their low chatter and cigarette smoke.

ALVY Thank you very much. It's a pleasure.

TONY *(Turning to introduce his entourage)* This is, uh, Shawn, and, uh . . . Bob and Petronia.

ANNIE Hi.

ENTOURAGE Hi.

ANNIE *(Laughing)* Hi, hi, Bob . . .

TONY Uh . . . w-we're going back to the Pierre. We're staying at the Pierre . . . and we're gonna meet Jack and Angelica, and have a drink there, and . . . if you'd like to come, uh, we'd love to have you.

ANNIE Yeah.

TONY And we could just sit and talk . . . nothing. Uh, not a big deal, it's just relax, just be very mellow.
Annie and Tony and his entourage turn to look at Alvy.

ALVY *(Fingers to his mouth, reacting)* Remember, we had that thing.

ANNIE What thing?

ALVY *(Staring at Annie and clearing his throat)* Don't you remember we-we-we discussed that thing that we were—

ANNIE *(Overlapping)* Thing?

ALVY *(Overlapping)* —yes, we had, uh . . .

ANNIE *(Looking at Alvy, reacting)* Oh, the thing! Oh, the thing . . . *(Laughing)* . . . yeah . . . yeah.
Annie turns, looks at Tony as he smiles and gestures with his hands.

TONY Oh, well, i-if it's inconvenient, eh, we can't do it now . . . that's fine, too. W-w-w-we'll do it another time.

ANNIE Hey—

TONY Maybe if you're on the Coast, we'll get together and . . . and we'll meet there.
He shakes hands with Annie.

ANNIE *(Reacting)* Oh.

TONY It was a wonderful set.

ANNIE Oh, gosh.

TONY *(Smiling)* I really enjoyed it. *(Looking at Alvy)* Nice to have metcha. Good night.

ENTOURAGE Bye-bye.

ANNIE Nice to see you . . . bye. Yeah. Bye.
She turns and looks at Alvy.

ALVY *(Reacting)* What's . . . you . . . well, what's the matter, wh— You w-wanna go to that party?

ANNIE *(Looking down at her hands, then up at Alvy)* I don't know, I thought it might be kind of fun, you know what I mean, it'd be nice to meet some new people.

ALVY *(Sighing)* I'm just not . . . you know, I don't think I could take a mellow eve— 'cause I-I don't respond well to mellow, you know what I mean, I-I have a tendency to . . . if I get too mellow, I-I ripen and then rot. You know, and it's—it's not good for my . . . *(Making sounds)*

ANNIE All right, all right, you don't wanna go to the party, so uh, whatta you wanna do?

INTERIOR. MOVIE THEATER.

The screen is projecting the beginning of The Sorrow and the Pity: *a street filled with fleeing cars, belongings tied on top and piled in the back seats. Subtitles pop on:*

> "The Jewish warmongers and
> Parisian plutocrats tried
> to flee with their gold and jewels"

as a narrator explains in German.

CUT TO:

Split screen: Annie and her psychiatrist on the left; Alvy and his on the right. Annie, talking, sits in a white molded chair, as does her doctor. The office is very modern: stark, white and chrome. Alvy, talking to his psychiatrist, lies on a deep leather sofa, the doctor seated away from him. This office looks more like a well-worn den: bookcases overflowing, dark wood. The dialogue is separated in each screen, though no one talks simultaneously.

ANNIE *(To her doctor)*   That day in Brooklyn was the last day I remember really having a great time.

ALVY *(To his doctor)*   Well, we never have any laughs anymore, is the problem.

ANNIE   Well, I've been moody and dissatisfied.

ALVY'S PSYCHIATRIST   How often do you sleep together?

ANNIE'S PSYCHIATRIST   Do you have sex often?

ALVY   Hardly ever. Maybe three times a week.

ANNIE   Constantly! I'd say three times a week. Like the other night, Alvy wanted to have sex.

ALVY She would not sleep with me the other night, you know, it's—

ANNIE And . . . I don't know . . . I mean, six months ago I-I woulda done it. I woulda done it, just to please him.

ALVY —I mean . . . I tried everything, you know, I-I-I put on soft music and my-my red light bulb, and . . .

ANNIE But the thing is—I mean, since our discussions here, I feel I have a right to my own feelings. I think you woulda been happy because . . . uh, uh, I really asserted myself.

ALVY The incredible thing about it is, I'm paying for her analysis and she's making progress and I'm getting screwed.

ANNIE I don't know, though, I feel so guilty because Alvy is paying for it, so, you know, so I do feel guilty if I don't go to bed with him. But if I do go to bed with him, it's like I'm going against my own feelings. I don't know—I-I can't win.

ALVY *(Simultaneously, with Annie)* You know . . . it's getting expensive . . . my analyst . . . for her analyst. She-she's making progress and I'm not making any progress. Her progress is defeating my progress.

ANNIE *(Simultaneously, with Alvy)* Sometimes I think—sometimes I think I should just live with a woman.

CUT TO:
INTERIOR. APARTMENT.

Alvy and Annie sit close together on the sofa in some friends' apartment. Their friends, another couple, stand behind the sofa in the background. Excited, they talk almost all at once.

WOMAN FRIEND Wow, I don't believe it . . . you mean to tell me you guys have never snorted coke?

ANNIE Well, I always wanted to try, you know, but, uh, Alvy, uh . . . he's very down on it.

ALVY Hey, don't put it on me. You kn— Wh-what is it, I don't wanna put a wad of white powder in my nose 'cause the-the nasal membranes . . .
They all start talking at once.

ANNIE You never wanna try anything new, Alvy.

ALVY *(Counting on his fingers)* How can you say that? I mean, *(Making sounds)* who said— I-I-I-I said that you, I and that girl from your acting class should sleep together in a threesome.

ANNIE *(Reacting)* That's sick!

ALVY Yeah, I know it's sick, but it's new. You know, you didn't say it couldn't be sick.
Annie laughs, chatters.

WOMAN FRIEND Just come on, Alvy. *(All four are now sitting on the sofa. The male friend starts to prepare lines of cocaine; Alvy and Annie look at each other, reacting)* Do your body a favor. Try it, come on.

ALVY Oh, yeah?

ANNIE Yeah. Come on. It'd be fun.

ALVY *(Moving forward on the couch)* Oh, I'm sure it's a lot of fun, 'cause the Incas did it, you know, and-and they-they-they were a million laughs.

ANNIE *(Laughing)* Alvy, come on, for your own experience. I mean, you wanna write, why not?

MALE FRIEND It's great stuff, Alvy. Friend of mine just brought it in from California.

ANNIE Oh, do you know something—I didn't tell yuh, we're going to California next week.

GIRL Oh, really?

ANNIE Yeah . . .

ALVY . . . I'm thrilled. As you know, uh . . . uh, on my agent's advice I sold out, and I'm gonna do an appearance on TV.

ANNIE *(Interrupting)* No, no, no that's not it at all. Alvy's giving an award on television. Gee, he talks like he's violating a moral issue sitting here.

GIRL You're kidding?

ALVY It's so phony, and we have to leave New York during Christmas week, which really kills me.

MAN *(Interrupting)* Alvy, listen, while you're in California, could you possibly score some coke for me?
Annie laughs.

ALVY *(Over Annie's laughter)* Sure, sure, I'll be glad to. I-I'll just put it in a-a-a h-h-hollow heel that I have in my boot, you know. *(Alvy picks up the small open gold case of cocaine the man has placed on the coffee table and looks at it, reacting)* H-h-how much is this stuff?

MAN It's about two thousand dollars an ounce.

ANNIE God.

ALVY Really? And what is the kick of it? Because I never . . .
He puts his finger into the drug, smells it and then sneezes. The powder blows all over the room as the man, woman and Annie react silently.

CUT TO:
CALIFORNIA. BEVERLY HILLS STREET—DAY.

It's a warm, beautiful day. Rob, Annie and Alvy in Rob's convertible are moving past the spacious houses, the palm trees. The sunlight reflects off the car. Annie, excited, is taking the whole place in. Background voices sing Christmas carols.

VOICES *(Singing)* We wish you a Merry Christmas,
We wish you a Merry Christmas
We wish you a Merry Christmas
And a Happy New Year.

ROB *(Over the singing)* I've never been so relaxed as I have been since I moved out here, Max. I want you to see my house. I live right next to Hugh Hefner's house, Max. He lets me use the Jacuzzi. And the women, Max, they're like the women in *Playboy* magazine, only they can move their arms and legs.

ANNIE *(Laughing)* You know, I can't get over that this is really Beverly Hills.

VOICES *(Singing)* We wish you a Merry Christmas
And a Happy New Year.

ALVY Yeah, the architecture is really consistent, isn't it? French next to—

VOICES *(Singing over the dialogue)*
Oh, Christmas . . . tree,
Oh, Christmas tree,
How bright and green
Our . . .

ALVY —Spanish, next to Tudor, next to Japanese.

ANNIE God, it's so clean out here.

ALVY It's that they don't throw their garbage away. They make it into television shows.

ROB Aw, come on, Max, give us a break, will yuh? It's Christmas.
Annie starts snapping pictures of the view.

ALVY Can you believe this is Christmas here?

VOICES *(Singing)* Oh Christmas tree,
                          Oh Christmas tree . . .
They pass a large house with spacious lawn. Sitting on the lawn is a Santa Claus complete with sleigh and reindeer. Voices continue to sing Christmas carols; Annie continues to take pictures.

ANNIE You know, it was snowing—it was snowing and really gray in New York yesterday.

ROB No kidding?

ALVY Right—well, Santa Claus will have sunstroke.

ROB Max, there's no crime, there's no mugging.

ALVY There's no economic crime, you know, but there's-there's ritual, religious-cult murders, you know, there's wheat-germ killers out here.

ROB While you're out here, Max, I want you to see some of my TV show. And we're invited to a big Christmas party.
They continue driving, now in a less residential area, passing a hot-dog stand. "Tail-Pup" concession; people mill about eating hot dogs.

VOICES *(Singing, louder now)*
                          Remember Christ our Savior
                          Was born on Christmas day
                          To save us all . . . from Satan's power
                          As we were gone astray.
They pass a theater, the marquee announcing "House of Exorcism Messiah of Evil. Rated R. Starts at 7:15."

INTERIOR. TV CONTROL ROOM.

Several monitors line the wall in front of an elaborate console. Rob and Alvy, along with Charlie, the technician, stand in the small room watching the screens showing Rob as a television star on a situation comedy. They chatter, analyzing the footage, over the sounds of the taped television comedy.

ALVY *(Overlapping the chatter)* Oh.

ROB Look, now, Charlie, give me a big laugh here.

ROB ON TV SCREEN A limousine to the track breakdown?

ROB *(Watching)* A little bigger.
TV monitors go black as the technician turns off the monitors to fix the laugh track.

ALVY Do you realize how immoral this all is?

ROB Max, I've got a hit series.

ALVY Yeah, I know, but you're adding fake laughs.
Technicians turn the monitors back on, showing Rob on the screen with another character, Arnie.

ARNIE Oh, I'm sorry.

ROB ON TV SCREEN Arnie.

ARNIE Yeah.

ROB *(Turning to the technician)* Give me a tremendous laugh here, Charlie.

ALVY Look, uh . . .
Loud laughter from the TV monitors.

ROB *(To Alvy)* We do the show live in front of an audience.

ALVY Great, but nobody laughs at it 'cause your jokes aren't funny.

ROB Yeah, well, that's why this machine is dynamite.

ROB ON TV SCREEN You better lie down. You've been in the sun too long.

ROB *(To the technician)* Yeah . . . uh, now give me a like a medium-size chuckle here . . . and then a big hand.
The sounds of laughter and applause are heard from the TV.

ALVY (*Removing his glasses and rubbing his face*) Is there booing on there?
The monitors show a woman on the screen.

WOMAN We were just gonna fix you up with my cousin Dolores.

ALVY (*Overlapping the TV*) Oh, Max, I don't feel well.

ROB What's the matter?

ALVY I don't know, I just got—I got very dizzy . . . (*Coughing*) I feel
dizzy, Max.

ROB Well, sit down.

ALVY (*Sitting down*) Oh, Jesus.

ROB You all right?

ALVY I don't know, I mean, I—

ROB (*Crouching before Alvy, looking at him*) You wanna lie down?

ALVY No, no—my, you know, my stomach felt queasy all morning.
I just started getting . . .

ROB How about a ginger ale?

ALVY Oh, Max . . . no, I—maybe I better lie down.

INTERIOR. HOTEL ROOM.

*Alvy lies in bed, one elbow propped up, a doctor sitting next to him looking
concerned. The doctor holds out a plate of chicken; Alvy listlessly stares at it.
Annie, in the background, is on the phone.*

ANNIE (*Talking into the phone*) Yes.

DOCTOR (*Holding out the food*) Why don't you just try to get a little of
this down? This is just plain chicken.

ALVY (*Taking a piece of chicken and holding it*) Oh, oh, no, I can't—I can't
eat this. I'm nauseous. (*He gasps and makes sounds*) If you could—if
you could just give me something to get me through the next two
hours, you know I-I have to go out to Burbank . . . and give out an
award on a TV show.

ANNIE (*On the phone, overlapping the doctor and Alvy*) Well . . . H-h huh
. . . Oh, good . . . Yes, I'll tell him.

DOCTOR Well, there's nothing wrong with you actually, so far as I can tell. I mean, you have no fever, no . . . no symptoms of anything serious. You haven't been eating pork or shellfish.
Annie hangs up and moves over to Alvy.

ANNIE *(Sitting on the edge of the bed)* Excuse me. I'm sorry, I'm sorry, Doctor. Uh, Alvy—Alvy, that was the show. They said everything is fine. They found a replacement, so they're going to tape without you.

ALVY *(Making sounds)* I'm nauseous. *(He sighs and gasps)* Oh, Jesus, now I don't get to do the TV show?
Reacting, Alvy puts up his hand in disgust, then starts eating the piece of chicken he has been holding. The doctor and Annie watch him, reacting.

ANNIE Yeah. Listen, Doctor, I'm worried.

DOCTOR Now, Mrs. Singer, I can't find anything—

ALVY Christ!

ANNIE Nothing at all?

DOCTOR No, I think I can get a lab man up here.

ALVY *(Grabbing the rest of the chicken from the plate)* Oh, Jesus. Can I have the salt, please?

ANNIE What do you mean? Do you think he's—

DOCTOR *(Handing the salt to Alvy)* Yes, excuse me. *(To Annie)* Perhaps it would be even better if we took him to the hospital for a day or two.
Alvy begins to eat.

ANNIE Uh-huh . . . Oh, hospital?

DOCTOR Well, otherwise, there's no real way to tell what's going on.

ALVY *(Making sounds, gasping)* This is not bad, actually.

EXTERIOR. BEVERLY HILLS STREET. RESIDENTIAL AREA—DAY.

Rob, Annie and Alvy in Rob's car pull into a long circular driveway as an attendant walks over to the car. A sprawling house is seen to the right; a couple moves toward the front door, and the driveway is crowded with other parked cars. Loud music is heard.

ALVY *(Getting out of the car)* Hey, don't tell me we're gonna hafta walk from the car to the house. Geez, my feet haven't touched pavement since I reached Los Angeles.

INTERIOR. HOUSE.

A Hollywood Christmas party is in session, complete with music, milling people, circulating waiters holding out trays of drinks. It's all very casual. French doors run the entire width of one wall; they are opened to the back lawn, guests move from the room to outside and back in. It is crowded; bits of conversation and clinking glasses can be heard. Two men, California-tanned, stand by the French doors talking.

1ST MAN Well, you take a meeting with him, I'll take a meeting with you if you'll take a meeting with Freddy.

2ND MAN I took a meeting with Freddy. Freddy took a meeting with Charlie. You take a meeting with him.

1ST MAN All the good meetings are taken.

CUT TO:
FULL GROUP SHOT.

A man stands talking, people in groups behind him. Two hornlike gadgets are attached to his shoulders; he's wearing a bizarre space costume.

3RD MAN Right now it's only a notion, but I think I can get money to make it into a concept . . . and later turn it into an idea.

CUT TO:

Alvy and Rob stand near the French doors leading to the back lawn, eating and drinking and watching the people walking in and out of the house.

ROB You like this house, Max?

ALVY M'hm.

ROB I even brought a road map to get us to the bathroom.

ALVY Whee, you shoulda told me it was Tony Lacey's party.

ROB What difference does that make?
Alvy looks into the room, where Annie and Tony Lacey are having an animated conversation.

ALVY   I think he has a little thing for Annie.

ROB   Oh, no, no, that's bullshit, Max. He goes with that girl over there.

ALVY   Where?
Rob nods his head toward a tall woman dressed all in white conversing with a group of people close-by.

ROB   The one with the V.P.L.

ALVY   V.P.L.?

ROB   Visible panty line. Max, she is gorgeous.

ALVY   Yeah, she's a ten, Max, and that's great for you because you're —you're used to twos, aren't you?

ROB   There are no twos, Max.

ALVY   Yeah, you're used to the kind with the—with the shopping bags walking through Central Park with the surgical masks on muttering.

ROB   M'hm.

ALVY   And . . . uh—

ROB *(Interrupting)*   How do you like this couple, Max?
A couple moves over toward Rob and Alvy. The man's arm is around the woman; they stand very close. In the background, Annie and Tony are still talking.

ROB   And I think they just came back from Masters and Johnson.

ALVY   Yeah, intensive care ward. *(Watching the woman in white)* My God—hey, Max, I think she's . . . I think she's giving me the eye.
As Rob and Alvy observe the guests, the woman in white starts walking toward them.

ROB   If she comes over here, Max, my brain is going to turn into guacamole.

ALVY   I'll handle it. I'll handle it. Hi.

GIRL IN WHITE   You're Alvy Singer, right? Didn't we meet at est?

ALVY *(Reacting)*   Est? No, no, I was never to est.

GIRL IN WHITE   Then how can you criticize it?

ALVY Oh.

ROB Oh, he—he didn't say anything.

ALVY *(Laughing)* No, no, I came out here to get some shock therapy, but there was an energy crisis, so I . . . He's my-my food taster. Have you two met?

ROB *(Shaking his head)* Hi. How do you do.

GIRL IN WHITE Do you taste to see if the food's poisoned?

ALVY Yeah, he's crazy.
The girl in white laughs.

ALVY *(Looking at Rob and the girl)* Hey, you guys are wearin' white. It must be in the stars.

ROB Yeah. Right.

ALVY Uri Geller must be on the premises someplace.

ROB We're gonna operate together.
Rob and the girl walk off together as the camera moves in on Tony and Annie standing by the buffet table.

TONY We just need about six weeks, in about six weeks we could cut a whole album.

ANNIE I don't know, this is strange to me, you know.

TONY Just . . . that's all you need. You can come and stay here.

ANNIE Oh.

TONY There's a whole wing in this house.

ANNIE *(Laughing)* Oh yeah, stay here? U-huh.

TONY You can have it to use. Why—why are you smiling?

ANNIE *(Laughing)* I don't know. I don't know.
She picks up an hors d'oeuvre.

CUT TO:

The two men still talking about meetings surrounded by other groups of people milling about.

IST MAN Not only is he a great agent, but he really gives good meetings.

2ND MAN   M'mm.

Tony, hand in hand with the girl in white, is leaving the party room with Alvy and Annie to show them the rest of the house.

TONY   This is a great house, really. Everything. Saunas, Jacuzzis, three tennis courts. You know who the original owners were? Nelson Eddy, then Legs Diamond. Then you know who lived here?

ALVY   Trigger.
Annie and the girl in white laugh.

TONY   Charlie Chaplin.

ALVY   Hey.

TONY   Right before his un-American thing.
They stop in a denlike screening room. A man is slouched back on one of the comfortable sofas that fill the room. It is much quieter in here; a contrast to the noise and crowd downstairs.

ALVY   Yeah, this place is great.

ANNIE   Yeah.

TONY   Uh, you guys are still—uh, you're still New Yorkers.

ALVY   Yeah, I love it there.

ANNIE   *(Laughing)*   Yeah.

TONY   Well, I used to live there. I used to live there for years. You know, but it's gotten—it's so dirty now.

ANNIE   Yeah.

ALVY   I'm into garbage. It's my thing.

ANNIE   Boy, this is really a nice screening room. It's really a nice room.

TONY   Oh, and there's another thing about New York. See . . . you-you wanna see a movie, you have to stand in a long line.

ANNIE   Yeah.

TONY   It could be freezing, it could be raining.

ANNIE   Yeah.

TONY And here, you just—

GIRL IN WHITE We saw *Grand Illusion* here last night.

ALVY AND ANNIE *(In unison)* Oh, yeah?

MAN ON THE SOFA *(Looking over his shoulder at the group)* That's a great film if you're high. *(The group laughs, looking down at the man on the sofa. He looks up at them, smiling, a joint in his hand, and offers them a cigarette)* Hey, you.

TONY *(Shaking his head no)* Come and see our bedroom. We did a fantastic lighting job. Okay?

ANNIE Oh, good. Okay.

ALVY I'm cool.
Tony and the girl in white leave the room, Annie and Alvy following.

ANNIE *(Taking Alvy's arm)* It's wonderful. I mean, you know they just watch movies all day.

ALVY Yeah, and gradually you get old and die. You know it's important to make a little effort once in a while.

ANNIE Don't you think his girl friend's beautiful?

ALVY Yeah, she's got a great-lookin' fa— A pat on the androgynous side. But it's . . .
They pass a man talking on the phone in the hallway.

MAN ON THE PHONE Yeah, yeah. I forgot my mantra.
As they come downstairs, the party is still in high gear. People are looser now; conversations are more animated, some talk quietly in more intimate corners, some couples are dancing. Alvy stands alone sipping a drink near the huge Christmas tree. A tall woman, passing by, shakes his hand, then leaves. He continues to sip his drink, alone, watching Tony and Annie in the center of the room dancing.
The screen shows a plane in flight, Los Angeles far below, then:

CUT TO:
AIRPLANE. INTERIOR.

Annie and Alvy sit, the stewardess behind them serving other passengers. Annie stares out the window holding a coffee cup; Alvy reads. Both are preoccupied, thinking their own thoughts.

ANNIE'S VOICE-OVER *(To herself)* That was fun. I don't think California is bad at all. It's a drag coming home.

ALVY'S VOICE-OVER *(To himself)* Lotta beautiful women. It was fun to flirt.

ANNIE'S VOICE-OVER *(As she sips coffee)* I have to face facts. I—I adore Alvy, but our relationship doesn't seem to work anymore.

ALVY'S VOICE-OVER *(An open magazine lies in his lap)* I'll have the usual trouble with Annie in bed tonight. Whatta I need this?

ANNIE'S VOICE-OVER If only I had the nerve to break up, but it would really hurt him.

ALVY'S VOICE-OVER If only I didn't feel guilty asking Annie to move out. It'd probably wreck her. But I should be honest.
He looks over at Annie.

ANNIE *(Looking back at Alvy)* Alvy, uh, let's face it. You know som— I don't think our relationship is working.

ALVY Tsch, I know. A relationship, I think, is-is like a shark, you know? It has to constantly move forward or it dies. *(He sighs)* And I think what we got on our hands *(Clearing his throat)* is a dead shark.

INTERIOR. ALVY'S LIVING ROOM—DAY.

A lighted Christmas tree stands in the middle of boxes, books, and the general disarray of packing and figuring out what belongs to whom as Alvy helps Annie move out.

ALVY *(Holding up a book)* Whose *Catcher in the Rye* is this?

ANNIE *(Walking into the room with an armload of books)* Well, let's see now . . . If it has my name on it, then I guess it's mine.

ALVY *(Reacting)* Oh, it sure has . . . You know, you wrote your name in all my books, 'cause you knew this day was gonna come.

ANNIE *(Putting down the books and flipping back her hair)* Well, uh, Alvy, you wanted to break up just as much as I do.

ALVY *(Riffling through the books)* There's no-no question in my mind. I think we're doing the mature thing, without any doubt.

ANNIE *(Holding a framed picture and moving about)* Now, look, all the books on death and dying are yours and all the poetry books are mine.

ALVY *(Looking down at a book)* This *Denial of Death*. You remember this?

ANNIE Oh—

ALVY This is the first book that I got you.
Annie goes over to Alvy. They both look down at the book; the fireplace, burning nicely, is behind them.

ANNIE —God.

ALVY Remember that day?

ANNIE Right. Geez, I feel like there's a great weight off my back. M'mmm.

ALVY Thanks, honey.

ANNIE *(Patting Alvy's shoulder)* Oh, no, no, no, no, no. I mean, you know, no, no, no, I mean, I think it's really important for us to explore new relationships and stuff like that.
She walks away.

ALVY There's no—there's no question about that, 'cause we've given this . . . uh, uh, I think a more than fair shot, you know?
He tosses the book into the carton.

ANNIE *(Offscreen)* Yeah, my analyst thinks this move is keen for me.

ALVY *(Offscreen)* Yeah, and I—an' I tru— you know, I trust her, because my-my analyst recommended her.

ANNIE *(Walking in with another armload of books)* Well, why should I put you through all my moods and hangups anyway?

ALVY Right. And you—and you know what the beauty part is?

ANNIE What?

ALVY *(Holding a small box of buttons)* We can always come back together again. Because there's no—there's no problem. 'Cause . . . Right.

ANNIE *(Overlapping)* Exactly, but . . . exactly. Ooooh!

ALVY You know, I-I-I don't think many couples could handle this. You know, they could just break up and remain friends.

ANNIE *(Taking a button from a box)* Hey, this one's mine, this button. This one, you rem—

ALVY *(Interrupting)* Yeah.

ANNIE I guess these are all yours. *Impeach,* uh, *Eisenhower . . . Impeach Nixon . . . Impeach Lyndon Johnson . . . Impeach Ronald Reagan.*

EXTERIOR. NEW YORK CITY. STREET—DAY.

People milling about on the sidewalk as Alvy walks out of a store and moves toward the foreground.

ALVY *(Into the camera, to the audience)* I miss Annie. I made a terrible mistake.
A couple, walking down the street, stops as the man talks to Alvy.

MAN ON THE STREET She's living in Los Angeles with Tony Lacey.

ALVY Oh, yeah? Well, if she is, then the hell with her! If she likes that lifestyle, let her live there! He's a jerk, for one thing.

MAN ON THE STREET He graduated Harvard.

ALVY Yeah. He may— Listen, Harvard makes mistakes too, you know. Kissinger taught there.
The couple strolls away as an older woman walks up to Alvy while others walk by.

OLD WOMAN Don't tell me you're jealous?

ALVY Yeah, jealous. A little bit like Medea. Lemme, lemme—can I show you something, lady? *(He takes a small item from his pocket to show the woman)* What I have here . . . I found this in the apartment. Black soap. She used to wash her face eight hundred times a day with black soap. Don't ask me why.

OLD WOMAN Well, why don't you go out with other women?

ALVY Well, I-I tried, but it's, uh, you know, it's very depressing.

RECENT FLASHBACK—INTERIOR. ALVY'S COUNTRY KITCHEN.

Alvy's arms and legs fill the screen as he slowly gets up from the floor holding up a live lobster. He puts it on a grill tray.

ALVY *(Pointing to the lobster)* This always happens to me. Quick, g-go get a broom.
His date, a girl wearing short shorts, leans against the sink and lights a cigarette. She makes no move to help.

GIRL DATE *(Smoking)* What are you making such a big deal about? *(As she talks, the lobster drops from the tray to the floor. Alvy jumps away, then gingerly scrapes the tray toward the lobster)* They're only lobsters. Look, you're a grown man, you know how to pick up a lobster.

ALVY *(Looking up in stooped-over position)* I'm not myself since I stopped smoking.

GIRL DATE *(Still leaning against the sink, her hand on her hip)* Oh, when'd you quit smoking?
He gets up off the floor with the lobster on the tray.

ALVY Sixteen years ago.

GIRL DATE *(Puzzled)* Whatta you mean?

ALVY *(Mocking)* Mean?

GIRL DATE You stopped smoking sixteen years ago, is that what you said? Oh, I-I don't understand. Are you joking, or what?

CUT TO:

A solitary Alvy walking along the FDR Drive where he had walked with Annie. The New York skyline is still in the background, the sea gulls go by, the foghorn blows. He walks slowly, moving offscreen.

INTERIOR. ALVY'S BEDROOM—DAY.

Alvy sits on his bed talking on the phone.

ALVY Listen, honey, Central Park's turning green . . . Yeah, I sa—I saw that lunatic that we—where we used to see . . . with the, uh, uh, pinwheel hat and, you know, and the roller skates? . . . Listen, I-I want you to come back here . . . Well, I-I—then I'm gonna come out there and getcha.

CUT TO:

An airborne plane.

CUT TO:
EXTERIOR. LOS ANGELES AIRPORT.

People milling about as Alvy, in the outside phone-booth center, talks.

ALVY Whatta you mean, where am I? Where do—where do you think I am? I'm-I'm out . . . I'm at the Los Angeles Airport. I flew in . . . *(Sniffling)* Tsch, I—well, I flew in to see you . . . *(Muttering)* Hey, listen, can we not debate this on-on the telephone because I'm, you know, I-I feel that I got a temperature and I'm-I'm getting my-my chronic Los Angeles nausea. I-I don't feel so good.
Alvy's conversation is still heard as the screen shows him behind the wheel of a car on a busy street; he causes a near-accident by jerking the car too slowly toward an intersection.

ALVY'S VOICE-OVER Well, where-wherever you wanna meet, I don't care. I'll-I'll drive in. I rented a car I'm driving . . . that . . . Whatta you mean? What—why is that such a miracle? I'm driving myself.

EXTERIOR. OUTDOOR CAFÉ—DAY.

People sit at umbrellaed tables with checkered tablecloths at a Sunset Boulevard outdoor café. Street traffic goes by while they dine. There's a mild California breeze. The restaurant is somewhat crowded as Alvy makes his way around the tables looking about. He finally sits down at an empty table; nearby sits a woman with a younger man. A waitress brings Alvy a menu and waits for his order.

ALVY *(To the waitress)* I'm gonna . . . I'm gonna have the alfalfa sprouts and, uh, a plate of mashed yeast.

Annie, wearing a flowered dress and wide hat, moves into view. Alvy, noticing her, watches as she walks over to his table. He rises and they shake hands.

ANNIE ' Hi.
Alvy wipes at his nose as he stares. He smiles, the street traffic moving behind him. Annie smiles back.

ALVY You look very pretty.

ANNIE Oh, no, I just lost a little weight, that's all. *(Alvy adjusts his glasses, not exactly knowing where to start; a bit uneasy)* Well, you look nice.

ALVY *(Nodding his head)* You see, I-I've been thinking about it and I think that we should get married.

ANNIE *(Adjusting her sunglasses)* Oh, Alvy, come on.

ALVY Why? You wanna live out here all year? It's like living in Munchkin Land.

ANNIE *(Looking around)* Well, whatta you mean? I mean, it's perfectly fine out here. I mean, Tony's very nice and, uh, well, I meet people and I go to parties and-and we play tennis. I mean, that's . . . that's a very big step for me, you know? I mean . . . *(Reacting, Alvy looks down at his hands, then up)* I'm able to enjoy people more.

ALVY *(Sadly)* So whatta you . . . You're not gonna come back to New York?

ANNIE *(Smiling)* What's so great about New York? I mean, it's a dying city. You read *Death in Venice.*

ALVY Hey, you didn't read *Death in Venice* till I bought it for yuh.

ANNIE That's right, that's right. *(Still smiling)* You only gave me books with the word "death" in the titles.

ALVY *(Nodding his head and gesturing)* That's right, 'cause it's an important issue.

ANNIE Alvy, you're incapable of enjoying life, you know that? I mean, your life is New York City. You're just this person. You're like this island unto yourself.

ALVY *(Toying with his car keys)* I can't enjoy anything unless I . . . unless everybody is. I—you know, if one guy is starving someplace, that's . . . you know, I-I . . . it puts a crimp in my evening. *(Looking down at his hands, sadly)* So wanna get married or what?

ANNIE *(Seriously)*   No. We're friends. I wanna remain friends.

ALVY *(In disbelief)*   Okay. *(Louder, to the waitress)* Check, please. Can I —can I . . .   Can I . . .   Can I . . .

ANNIE *(Interrupting)*   You're mad, aren't you?

ALVY *(Shaking his head)*   No. *(Then nodding)* Yes, of course I'm mad, because you love me, I know that.

ANNIE   Alvy, I can't say that that's true at this point in my life. I really just can't say that that's true. I mean, you know how wonderful you are. I mean, you know . . . you're the reason that I got outta my room and that I was able to sing, and-and-and, you know, get more in touch with my feelings and all that crap. Anyway, look, I don't wanna— Listen, listen, listen, uh *(Laughing)* h'h, so whatta you up to anyway, huh?

ALVY *(Shrugging his shoulders)*   The usual, you know. Uh, tryin' t' write. I'm workin' on a play. *(Sighing)* Jesus. So whatta yuh saying? That you're not comin' back to New York with me?
He nods his head in disbelief.

ANNIE *(Nodding)*   No! *(Pauses)* Look, I gotta go.
She starts to rise.

ALVY   You mean that . . . *(He gets up and starts following her past diners at other tables)* I-I-I-I flew three thousand miles to see you.

ANNIE   I'm late.

ALVY   Air miles, you know. I mean, you know what that does to my stomach?
They move down the steps of the café toward the parking lot.

ANNIE   If you must know, it's a hectic time for Tony. The Grammys are tonight.

ALVY   The what?

ANNIE   The Grammys. He's got a lotta records up for awards.

ALVY   You mean they give awards for that kind o' music.

ANNIE   Oh!

ALVY I thought just earplugs.
Annie gets into her car. Alvy moves over to his rented convertible.

ANNIE Just forget it, Alvy, okay? Let's just forget the conversation.
She closes the door, starts the motor.

ALVY *(Yelling after her)* Awards! They do nothing but give out awards!
I can't believe it. Greatest, greatest fascist dictator, Adolf Hitler!
Annie drives away.
*Alvy gets behind the wheel, starts the motor. Putting the car in gear, he
inadvertently moves forward, hitting a bunch of trash cans with a loud crash.
Putting the car in reverse, Alvy notices a beige car that has just turned into
the parking lot.*
*For a brief moment, the screen shows a flashback of the bumper-car ride at
the Brooklyn amusement park. Alvy's father is on the platform directing
traffic; young Alvy is in a small car bumping others right and left.*
*Alvy, back in the parking lot, backs up his convertible, purposefully smashing
the side of the beige car as another flashback of bumper-car ride appears, this
time—as Alvy's father directs traffic—a Marine in a small car hits the back
end of a soldier's car, and Alvy, back in the parking lot, moves his car over
to another parked car and hits it full force.*
*Another flashback appears: people in the small cars really racing around the
track now, bumping into one another over and over again, Alvy's father
directing the flow, as the film cuts back to the parking lot, where Alvy reverses
the convertible and rams it into the front end of yet another car.*
*He sits behind the wheel as people rush out of various cars and as sirens start
blaring, coming closer and closer, stopping finally as a motorcycle cop gets
off beside Alvy's car and walks over to him)*

ALVY *(Getting out of the car)* Officer, I know what you're gonna say.
I'm-I'm not a great driver, you know, I-I have some problems with-
with-with—

OFFICER *(Interrupting)* May I see your license, please?

ALVY Sure. *(Searching, he finally fishes his license out of his pocket)* Just
don't-don't get angry, you know what I mean. 'Cause I-I have—I
have my-my license here. You know, it's a rented car. And I-I-I-I-
I've . . .
He drops the license and it falls to the ground.

OFFICER Don't give me your life story *(Looking at the piece of paper on
the ground)*—just pick up the license.

ALVY Pick up the license. You have to ask nicely 'cause I've had an extremely rough day. You know, my girl friend—

OFFICER *(Interrupting)* Just give me the license, please.

ALVY Since you put it that way. *(He laughs)* It's hard for me to refuse. *(He leans over, picks up the license, then proceeds to rip it up. He lets the pieces go; they float to the ground)* . . . have a, I have a terrific problem with authority, you know. I'm . . . it's not your fault. Don't take it personal.

CUT TO:
INTERIOR. JAIL-CELLS CORRIDOR.

A guard moves down the hall to the cell where Alvy stands with other inmates. He unlocks the door and opens it, letting Alvy out.

ALVY So long, fellas. Keep in touch.
He walks down the corridor offscreen.

EXTERIOR. A STREET IN FRONT OF THE COURTHOUSE—DAY.

Policemen are walking up and down the courthouse steps as Alvy and Rob move out the door of the building, down the steps to the street.

ROB Imagine my surprise when I got your call, Max.

ALVY *(Carrying his jacket over his shoulder)* Yeah. I had the feeling that I got you at a bad moment. You know, I heard high-pitched squealing.
They walk over to Rob's convertible and get in.

ROB *(Starting the car)* Twins, Max. Sixteen-year-olds. Can you imagine the mathematical possibilities?

ALVY *(Reacting)* You're an actor, Max. You should be doing Shakespeare in the Park.

ROB Oh, I did Shakespeare in the Park, Max. I got mugged. I was playing Richard the Second and two guys with leather jackets stole my leotard.
He puts on an elaborate helmet and goggles.

ALVY *(Looking at Rob's helmet)* Max, are we driving through plutonium?

ROB Keeps out the alpha rays, Max. You don't get old.

CUT TO:
INTERIOR. REHEARSAL HALL OF A THEATER.

An actor and actress sit on hard wooden chairs in a sparse rehearsal hall. They face each other. The actress resembles Annie; the actor, Alvy.

ACTOR   You're a thinking person. How can you choose this lifestyle?

ACTRESS   What is so incredibly great about New York? It's a dying city! You-you read *Death in Venice.*

ACTOR   You didn't read *Death in Venice* till I gave it to you!

ACTRESS   Well, you only give me books with the word "death" in the title.
The camera pulls back, showing Alvy sitting with two men at a table set up near the actors. A mirror, running the whole width of the wall, reflects the two actors, a script lying on the table between them. It is obvious now that they are rehearsing a scene that Alvy wrote.

ACTOR   *(In mirrored reflection)*   It's an important issue.

ACTRESS   *(In mirrored reflection)*   Alvy, you are totally incapable of enjoying life.
The camera moves back to actual actor and actress.

ACTRESS   You're like New York. You're an island.

ACTOR   *(Rising with emotion)*   Okay, if that's all that we've been through together means to you, I guess it's better if we just said goodbye, once and for all! You know, it's funny, after all the se-rious talks and passionate moments that it ends here . . . in a health-food restaurant on Sunset Boulevard. Goodbye, Sunny.
The actor begins to leave as the actress jumps up from her chair.

ACTRESS   Wait! I'm-I'm gonna . . . go with you. *(The actor comes back. They embrace)* I love you.
The camera cuts to Alvy, who turns and looks straight into the camera.

ALVY   *(To the audience, gesturing)*   Tsch, whatta you want? It was my first play. You know, you know how you're always tryin' t' get things to come out perfect in art because, uh, it's real difficult in life. Interestingly, however, I did run into Annie again. It was on the Upper West Side of Manhattan.
Annie, singing "Seems Like Old Times," overlaps Alvy's speech and continues over the next scene, where Alvy, standing in front of a Manhattan theater, shakes hands with Annie and her escort. The theater marquee reads "OPHULS PRIZE FILM THE SORROW AND THE PITY."

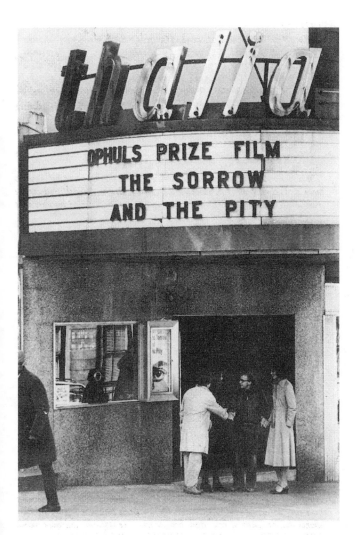

ALVY'S VOICE *(Over the theater scene and Annie's singing)* She had moved back to New York. She was living in SoHo with some guy. *(Laughing)* And when I met her she was, of all things, dragging him in to see *The Sorrow and the Pity.* Which I counted as a personal triumph. Annie and I . . . *(Alvy's voice continues over the scene shot through a window of Manhattan café showing Alvy and Annie sitting at a table, laughing and enjoying themselves)* . . . we had lunch sometime after that, and, uh, just, uh, kicked around old times.

A series of flashbacks following in quick succession while Annie continues to sing:

Annie and Alvy going up the FDR Drive, the day they met playing tennis, Annie driving, Alvy holding up partially eaten sandwich.

Annie and Alvy in the Hamptons house kitchen, Annie handing a live lobster to Alvy, who drops it in the pot on the stove.

Annie and Alvy walking side by side by the shoreline.

Alvy at the tennis club, packing his bag, as he looks over his shoulder and sees Annie, hands on her face, then clapping, as she offers him a ride home in her car.

Annie opening the door to Alvy the night he came over to kill the spider; Annie and Alvy in the bookstore buying the "Death" titles; Annie and Alvy in their Hamptons house, Annie reading a school catalogue, the night Alvy puts in the red light.

The memories continue to flash on the screen: Annie and Alvy at a friend's house, Alvy blowing the cocaine all over the sofa; Annie and Alvy playing tennis; Annie and Alvy having a picture taken backstage at the college performance in Annie's hometown; Alvy holding Annie close, the night he came over to kill the spider.

And continue: Annie carrying her luggage and clothes into Alvy's bedroom, Alvy following, the day she first moved into his apartment. Annie holding up her sexy birthday present from Alvy, then leaning over and kissing him; Annie and Alvy walking down a city street, holding each other close; sitting on the park bench, observing the people; and kissing, on the FDR Drive, the New York City skyline behind them.

The music stops.

Returning to the present, the camera, focusing through the café window, shows Annie and Alvy across street. They look about at the city traffic. Lunch is over; it's time.

Alvy and Annie shake hands and kiss each other friendly like. Annie crosses the street, Alvy watching her go. Then he turns, and slowly walks down the street offscreen. His voice is heard over the scene:

ALVY'S VOICE-OVER   After that it got pretty late. And we both hadda go, but it was great seeing Annie again, right? I realized what a terrific person she was and-and how much fun it was just knowing her and I-I thought of that old joke, you know, this-this-this guy goes to a psychiatrist and says, "Doc, uh, my brother's crazy. He thinks he's a chicken." And, uh, the doctor says, "Well, why don't you turn him in?" And the guy says, "I would, but I need the eggs." Well, I guess that's pretty much how how I feel about relationships. You know, they're totally irrational and crazy and absurd and . . . but, uh, I guess we keep goin' through it because, uh, most of us need the eggs.

THE END

DISSOLVES INTO:
BLACK BACKGROUND; credits popping on and off in white.

Credits

Production Manager	ROBERT GREENHUT
1st Assistant Director	FRED T. GALLO
2nd Assistant Director	FRED BLANKFEIN
Location Manager	MARTIN DANZIG
Script Supervisor	KAY CHAPIN
Production Office Co-ordinator	LOI KRAMER
Assistant to Mr. Allen	PATRICIA CROWN
Location Auditor	SAM GOLDRICH
Transportation Captain	WILLIAM CURRY
D.G.A. Trainee	TAD DEVLIN
Production Assistants	CHRIS CRONYN
	BETH RUDIN
	STUART SMILEY
Sound Mixer	JAMES SABAT
Re-recording Mixer	JACK HIGGINS
Camera Operator	FRED SCHULER
1st Assistant Cameraman	THOMAS PRIESTLY
Gaffer	DUSTY WALLACE
Key Grip	ROBERT WARD
Wardrobe Supervisor	GEORGE NEWMAN
Wardrober Supervisor	MARILYN PUTNAM
Makeup Artist	FERN BUCHNER
Unit Publicist	SCOTT MACDONOUGH
Still Photographer	BRIAN HAMILL
Set Decorators	ROBERT DRUMHELLER
	JUSTIN SCOPPA JR.
Propmaster	THOMAS SACCIO
Carpenter	JOSEPH BADALUCCO
Scenic Artist	COSMO SORICE
Construction Grip	JOSEPH WILLIAMS
Film Editor	WENDY GREEN BRICMONT
Assistant Film Editors	SONYA POLANSKI
	SUSAN E. MORSE
Sound Editing	SAN SABLE/MAGNOFEX
Video Services	E.U.E/SCREEN GEMS
Titles	COMPUTER OPTICALS
Casting	JULIET TAYLOR
Extra Casting	AARON BECKWITH
Clothing Designed By	RALPH LAUREN
Animated Sequences	CHRIS ISHII
Miss Keaton's Accompanist	ARTIE BUTLER

Los Angeles Unit:
  Location Manager   DAISY GERBER
  Camera Operator   DON THORIN
  Sound Mixer   JAMES PILCHER
  Gaffer   LARRY HOWARD
  Key Grip   CARL GIBSON
  Transportation Captain   JAMES FOOTE
  Set Decorator   BARBARA KRIEGER
  Propmaster   PAT O'CONNOR
  Makeup   JOHN INZERELLA
  Hair Stylist   VIVIENNE WALKER
  Wardrobe Supervisor   NANCY MCARDLE
Songs   "SEEMS LIKE OLD TIMES"
  Music by   CARMEN LOMBARDO
  Lyrics by   JOHN JACOB LOEB
            "IT HAD TO BE YOU"

  Music by   ISHAM JONES
  Lyrics by   GUS KAHN

CAST
Woody Allen   ALVY SINGER
Diane Keaton   ANNIE HALL
Tony Roberts   ROB
Carol Kane   ALLISON
Paul Simon   TONY LACEY
Shelley Duvall   PAM
Janet Margolin   ROBIN
Colleen Dewhurst   MOM HALL
Christopher Walken   DUANE HALL
Donald Symington   DAD HALL
Helen Ludlam   GRAMMY HALL
Mordecai Lawner   ALVY'S DAD
Joan Newman   ALVY'S MOM
Jonathan Munk   ALVY AGED 9
Ruth Volner   ALVY'S AUNT
Martin Rosenblatt   ALVY'S UNCLE
Hy Ansel   JOEY NICHOLS
Rashel Novikoff   AUNT TESSIE
Russell Horton   MAN IN THEATER LINE
Marshall McLuhan   HIMSELF
Christine Jones   DORRIE

- - -

Mary Boylan	MISS REED
Wendy Girard	JANET
John Doumanian	COKE FIEND
Bob Maroff	MAN #1 OUTSIDE THEATER
Rick Petrucelli	MAN #2 OUTSIDE THEATER
Lee Callahan	TICKET SELLER AT THEATER
Chris Gampel	DOCTOR
Dick Cavett	HIMSELF
Mark Lenard	NAVY OFFICER
Dan Ruskin	COMEDIAN AT RALLY
John Glover	ACTOR BOYFRIEND
Bernie Styles	COMIC'S AGENT
Johnny Haymer	COMIC
Ved Bandhu	MAHARISHI
John Dennis Johnson	L.A. POLICEMAN
Lauri Bird	TONY LACEY'S GIRL FRIEND
Jim McKrell	LACEY PARTY GUEST
Jeff Goldblum	LACEY PARTY GUEST
William Callaway	LACEY PARTY GUEST
Roger Newman	LACEY PARTY GUEST
Alan Landers	LACEY PARTY GUEST
Jean Sarah Frost	LACEY PARTY GUEST
Vince O'Brien	HOTEL DOCTOR
Humphrey Davis	ALVY'S PSYCHIATRIST
Veronica Radburn	ANNIE'S PSYCHIATRIST
Robin Mary Paris	ACTRESS IN REHEARSAL
Charles Levin	ACTOR IN REHEARSAL
Wayne Carson	REHEARSAL STAGE MANAGER
Michael Karm	REHEARSAL DIRECTOR
Petronia Johnson	TONY'S DATE AT NIGHTCLUB
Shaun Casey	TONY'S DATE AT NIGHTCLUB
Ricardo Bertoni	WAITER #1 AT NIGHTCLUB
Michael Aronin	WAITER #2 AT NIGHTCLUB
Lou Picetti	STREET STRANGER
Loretta Tupper	STREET STRANGER
James Burge	STREET STRANGER
Shelley Hack	STREET STRANGER
Albert Ottenheimer	STREET STRANGER
Paula Trueman	STREET STRANGER
Beverly D'Angelo	ACTRESS IN ROB'S TV SHOW
Tracey Walter	ACTOR IN ROB'S TV SHOW

David Wier	ALVY'S CLASSMATE
Kieth Dentice	ALVY'S CLASSMATE
Susan Mellinger	ALVYS CLASSMATE
Hamit Perezic	ALVY'S CLASSMATE
James Balter	ALVY'S CLASSMATE
Eric Gould	ALVY'S CLASSMATE
Amy Levitan	ALVY'S CLASSMATE
Gary Allen	SCHOOLTEACHER
Frank Vohs	SCHOOLTEACHER
Margaretta Warwick	SCHOOLTEACHER
Lucy Lee Flippen	WAITRESS AT HEALTH-FOOD RESTAURANT
Gary Muledeer	MAN AT HEALTH-FOOD RESTAURANT
Sigourney Weaver	ALVY'S DATE OUTSIDE THEATER
Walter Bernstein	ANNIE'S DATE OUTSIDE THEATER

Recorded Music:

"A Hard Way to Go"
Performed by Tim Weisberg on A&M Records

Christmas Medley
Performed by the Do-Re-Mi Children's Chorus
on Vocalion Records

"Sleepy Lagoon"
Performed by Tommy Dorsey on RCA Records